W9-CBP-023

FREDERICK BUECHNER

Novelist/Theologian of the Lost and Found

FREDERICK BUECHNER

Novelist/Theologian of the Lost and Found

by Marjorie Casebier McCoy
with Charles S. McCoy

1817

Harper & Row, Publishers, San Francisco

Cambridge, Hagerstown, New York, Philadelphia, Washington
London, Mexico City, São Paulo, Singapore, Sydney

Acknowledgment is made to Harper & Row, Publishers, Inc., and to Atheneum Publishers, an imprint of Macmillan Publishing Company, for use of excerpts from books by Frederick Buechner. From Harper & Row: *The Alphabet of Grace,* copyright © 1970 by Frederick Buechner; *The Final Beast, copyright* © 1965 by Frederick Buechner; *The Magnificent Defeat,* copyright © 1966 by Frederick Buechner; *Now and Then,* copyright © 1983 by Frederick Buechner; *A Room Called Remember,* copyright © 1984 by Frederick Buechner; *The Sacred Journey,* copyright © 1982 by Frederick Buechner; and *Telling the Truth,* copyright © 1977 by Frederick Buechner. From Atheneum: *The Book of Bebb,* copyright © 1979 by Frederick Buechner.

The poem on p. 152 is excerpted from *The Fellowship of the Ring* of *The Lord of the Rings* by J. R. R. Tolkien. Copyright © 1965 by J. R. R. Tolkien. Reprinted by permission of Houghton Mifflin Company and Unwin Hyman Limited.

Library of Congress Cataloging-in-Publication Data

McCoy, Marjorie Casebier
   Frederick Buechner: novelist/theologian of the lost and found.

   Includes index.
   1. Buechner, Frederick.
2. Novelists, American—20th century—Biography.
3. Theologians—United States—Biography.
4. Theology in literature. I. McCoy, Charles S.
II. Title.
PS3552.U35Z78   1988   813'.54 [B]
ISBN 0-06-065329-9   87-45712

88 89 90 91 92 RRD 10 9 8 7 6 5 4 3 2 1

For
my husband, Charles,
my sisters, Jo and Pat,
and my friend Elizabeth

Contents

Preface

Writing this book has been for me a process of feeling my way into words. Buechner says of his novels that they begin with a "lump in my throat." That is where my response to Buechner's work had its starting point in my own awareness. It began with a lump in my throat—a lump evoked by Buechner's way with words—and with a passion to articulate what the experience of reading his words and coming to dwell in his characters, situations, and stories has meant to me. My hope is that, as I tell what has happened to me, others will be drawn into Buechner's circle of readers and, like me, find their lives enriched and deepened.

Insofar as the stories of our own faith and life can be contained and communicated through written accounts of those events that have shaped us, these pages tell how Buechner's experience, as it emerges in his writing, has become part of my own story, my own self. Feeling my way into the words that have found their way onto these pages has been, therefore, as much a means of self-discovery as it has been a means of finding ways to express my understanding of him.

It occurred to me that, if I could come close to describing *what it was I had experienced* through reading Frederick Buechner's books, I would come close to understanding what had happened to me. If not, then I must remain in the dark about why I had been weeping or laughing or shaking my head, sometimes with sudden insight, sometimes with amazement! I went back through all my notes on Buechner, rereading sections that had seemed to leap off his pages and into my mind, meditating on those passages that had struck chords deep within me—not *lost* chords so much as ones that can never be completely *duplicated*.

What has emerged in these pages is both less than I had hoped for and also far more. It is less than I had anticipated as a complete

account of the depth of *my* experience of Buechner's writing. But it is
more than I had dared hope as a summary of what I perceive to be
Buechner's experience.

I want to express my continuing appreciation to students in a class
I taught on Frederick Buechner at Pacific School of Religion in Berkeley. They joined me in an exciting journey through the varied and wondrous landscape of his books and threw themselves into the enterprise
with Bebbsian enthusiasm and joy. They responded in ways that
revealed to me and to themselves unexpected dimensions of Buechner's
work. The process also opened up undiscovered territory in their own
lives, as it did in mine. My students educated me at least as much as
I taught them. Perhaps it is better to say that Buechner taught us all.
The pages that follow owe a great deal to our mutual learning in the
class as we shared what Buechner evoked in us and we came out of the
shadows of our isolated selves to dance together around the bonfire-
brightness of his stories.

Helpful also in clarifying my thinking about Buechner and giving
me the courage to believe that I might be able to make a contribution
by writing this book was the class on Buechner that my husband,
Charles, and I led at the Earl Lectures and Pastoral Conference at
Pacific School of Religion in 1983. Frederick Buechner was one of the
major speakers. It was a little unnerving, as we prepared to begin the
first session, to see the subject of our discussion slip unobtrusively into
the back row of the large room in which we were meeting. His presence
probably made us more consciously responsible in dealing with those
of his writings we were using to explain the experiences out of which
his work came. And his gracious response to our presentation nudged
me toward attempting this book.

I hope that all those who read this account of what I have seen
in Buechner and discovered about the meaning of my own life from
him will be led to his writings and be helped by what I had found in
his stories to understand their own lives better and to express their own
stories with greater satisfaction and joy.

While working on this manuscript, I developed some strange
symptoms that were diagnosed as a malignant brain tumor. Buechner's
encounters with death and his awareness of growing old and living
with the expectation of dying have struck me with a special and personal

force as I have reread the novels within the context of my own illness. Lucille Bebb has come closer to me. Godric at times has seemed to climb into my own skin and live within me. Antonio Parr and his twin sister, Miriam, who has cancer, have whispered in my ear. Trying to complete this book with those characters for company has become as much therapy as achievement.

Many people have helped along the way. Elizabeth Berryhill has been a partner in the process of bringing inklings and images to expression. This manuscript would never have made its way to my editor's desk without the careful and patient work of my companion in love, Charles. He has made sense of my writing, sorted out what could be used from what I had told him, listened to tapes to fill in gaps, and checked with students to clarify comments I had made.

What all of us have accomplished together has helped change difficult days into times of wonder and joy. I am grateful for these companions on our sacred journey together.

Marjorie Casebier McCoy
Berkeley, California

Books by Frederick Buechner
with Abbreviations Used

When I quote from any of Buechner's books, which follow, I use the abbreviation that appears in parentheses after the title.

FICTION:

A Long Day's Dying (LDD). New York: Knopf, 1950.
The Seasons' Difference (SD). New York: Knopf, 1952.
The Return of Ansel Gibbs (RAG). New York: Knopf, 1958.
The Final Beast (FB). New York: Atheneum, 1965.
The Entrance to Porlock (EP). New York: Atheneum, 1970.
Lion Country (LC). New York: Atheneum, 1971.
Open Heart (OH). New York: Atheneum, 1972.
Love Feast (LF). New York: Atheneum, 1974.
Treasure Hunt (TH). New York: Atheneum, 1977.
The Book of Bebb: Lion Country, Open Heart, Love Feast, Treasure Hunt (BB). New York: Atheneum, 1979.
Godric (G). New York: Atheneum, 1981.
Brendan. New York: Atheneum, 1987. (Not given attention in this volume.)

NONFICTION:

The Magnificent Defeat (MD). New York: Seabury, 1966.
The Hungering Dark (HD). New York: Seabury, 1969.
The Alphabet of Grace (AG). New York: Seabury, 1970.

Wishful Thinking: A Theological ABC (*WT*). New York: Harper & Row, 1973.

The Faces of Jesus (*FJ*). Croton-on-Hudson, N.Y.: Riverwood Publishers, 1974. (Titled *The Life of Jesus* in later editions.)

Telling the Truth: The Gospel as Tragedy, Comedy, and Fairy Tale (*TT*). San Francisco: Harper & Row, 1977.

Peculiar Treasures: A Biblical Who's Who (*PT*). San Francisco: Harper & Row, 1979.

A Room Called Remember: Uncollected Pieces (*RCR*). San Francisco: Harper & Row, 1984.

Whistling in the Dark: An ABC Theologized. San Francisco: Harper & Row, 1988. (Published while this volume was in press.)

AUTOBIOGRAPHY:

The Sacred Journey (*SJ*). San Francisco: Harper & Row, 1982.
Now and Then (*NT*). San Francisco: Harper & Row, 1983.

"Among Confession, and Tears, and Great Laughter"

> Every once in a while life can be very eloquent. You go along from day to day not noticing very much, not seeing or hearing very much, and then all of a sudden, when you least expect it very often, something speaks to you with such power that it catches you off guard, makes you listen whether you want to or not. Something speaks to you out of your own life with such directness that it is as if it calls you by name and forces you to look where you have not had the heart to look before, to hear something that maybe for years you have not had the wit or the courage to hear. (*RCR*, 13)

Frederick Buechner is telling us about important moments in his own life. But that is only part of the truth. He is also telling the rest of us something crucial about ourselves and what often happens to us. Like an arrow aimed between our eyes, a sentence gets our attention. When it hits us we dissolve into relief and laughter as its rubber suction cup makes it stick.

His writing has a compelling quality for me and many others because it emerges from those times in his life that have forced him to listen. Before we know it we find ourselves paying attention first to him and then to our own experience. He speaks from the depth of his own life to the depth of ours.

In his autobiographical and nonfiction works, Buechner speaks *directly* of those eloquent moments in his life so that we have the sense of being transported into his experience and brought to share it with him. His novels come from the same sources at the center of his life and draw us into their world with the same power. In his fiction the themes are presented *indirectly* in forms sometimes still recognizable as from his own experience, yet transmuted by his imagination as an artist. In either case, directly or indirectly, he demonstrates the ability to speak to us and our own experience, to make us listen, and to confront us with new insights about ourselves as loving, hoping, suffering, believing human beings. The ways he manages to work these miracles within us disclose his gifts as artist and as theologian.

It was in 1965 that I first discovered Buechner. My initial encounter was through a review of his novel *The Final Beast*.[1] The review was by Amos Wilder, a New Testament scholar and well-known poet, who has written with great perceptiveness on the relation of theology and literature. He is the brother of novelist and playwright Thornton Wilder.

What Amos Wilder had to say about Buechner's novel intrigued me so much that I had to read it for myself. Doing that was enough to hook me hopelessly and finally. Since then I have read all of Buechner's books and most of his articles and interviews. I have also had opportunities to hear him speak and to discuss his work with him. The process of getting acquainted with Buechner the novelist, theologian, and human being has been a continuing experience of discovery and self-discovery.

Over the years since his first book was published in 1950, Buechner has produced an impressive collection of novels, a total of eleven to date. More amazing than the quantity, however, is the fantastic array of characters he sets before us, the varied settings these characters inhabit, and the depth of feeling and meaning his writing can evoke in his readers.

The Final Beast was the book of Buechner's that I read first. I found in it a stunning story of a preacher in a small New England town, struggling with the death of his wife the previous year, trying to take care of his children while performing his pastoral duties, facing the threat of a sex scandal, and seeking the meaning of his own faith and vocation. The human sensitivity and theological profundity with which Buechner handled the plot and the people demonstrated an integration of art and religion that I found irresistible.

After I had completed this remarkable book, and reread it to absorb further its rich imagery and pulsing faith, I set out to learn about the person who could write such a story. The information on the dust jacket gave me a beginning. There I discovered that he was a Presbyterian minister serving as school minister and teacher of religion at Phillips Exeter Academy, a boy's secondary school in New Hampshire, and had written three novels before *The Final Beast*. With a little more investigation, I found out what I had already guessed. He had gone through considerable inner turmoil and change before coming to the depth of Christian faith that appeared through the characters and events of this story that had impressed me so deeply. It was clear to me that I had to read more.

A close friend had also been smitten with Buechner after reading Wilder's review of *The Final Beast* and the novel itself. Together we searched out the novels he had already published and watched for new works of his to appear. It did not surprise us that the next book was made up of meditations based on sermons Buechner had given at Phillips Exeter Academy in his role as school minister. *The Magnificent Defeat* has all the style and power of *The Final Beast* and has always seemed to me to be a direct statement of what emerges more indirectly in the novel. Those sermons might have been delivered by Theodore Nicolet, the preacher in *The Final Beast*.

Not long thereafter, my friend and I located his first two novels, *A Long Day's Dying* (1950) and *The Seasons' Difference* (1952). Both are superbly crafted and demonstrate the same excellence of style that are hallmarks of Buechner's writing, but the atmosphere and perspective are very different. These early books depict a mood of sophisticated modernity, with a narrator at an omniscient, disinterested distance from the action. Even so, there are indications of religious concern that will surface later. The first novel focuses on a priestlike figure named Tristram Bone, draws its title and perhaps more than one of its characters from Milton's *Paradise Lost*, and explores the complexities of human relations, with their tangle of faith and faithlessness. The second novel recounts the rippling impact and varied reactions when a young teacher reports that he has had a religious vision. Though quite different in theme, setting, and action from his later writing, these first novels reflect a serious depth of religious seeking and moral probing that foreshadow the direction Buechner's life would take.

His third novel, *The Return of Ansel Gibbs* (1958), deals with the deepened human sensitivity and commitment that events force upon a stoic public figure recalled from retirement to join the president's cabinet. I found it especially interesting, not only because it showed Buechner growing toward the theological vision and understanding that characterized his later work, but also because an important character was modeled on a professor whom I knew and admired, James

Muilenburg, who was then teaching at Union Theological Seminary in New York and was later to teach at the Graduate Theological Union in Berkeley. Buechner was profoundly affected by this great Old Testament scholar and teacher, dedicating his first book of meditations, *The Magnificent Defeat*, to Muilenburg.

By this time I was thoroughly addicted to Buechner and awaited eagerly each new wonder, novelistic or other, that came from his pen. The next book was another collection of meditations, *The Hungering Dark* (1969), this one dedicated "To My Former Students and Colleagues at the Phillips Exeter Academy," which he had left in 1967 to devote himself full-time to writing. If I understand Buechner's intention, the dedication was well directed. Following the German theologian Friedrich Schleiermacher, Buechner in his sermons had been attempting to reach out to the "cultured despisers of religion." The students and faculty at Phillips Exeter had been, for the most part, just that when he had arrived at the school, and it had been they who compelled him to hone his preaching and literary skills to their utmost in order to get a hearing for Christian faith. As I shall suggest later, the academy's students and faculty played an important role in Buechner's development.

His fifth novel, *The Entrance to Porlock*, was published in 1970. Again, it was different but still displayed the virtuoso talent to which I had become accustomed. I was entranced with this artful retelling of *The Wizard of Oz*. Related with compelling warmth and engaging fantasy, the story is about an old man, his two middle-aged sons, and his grandson, who go on a journey together, each seeking something to complete his identity, as was the case with Dorothy, the Scarecrow, the Tin Woodman, and the Cowardly Lion when they set off down the Yellow Brick Road toward the Emerald City.

About this time Buechner increased his productivity. He began writing faster than I could read. But it was worth it trying to keep up with him. He gave the Noble Lectures at Harvard in 1969, subsequently published as *The Alphabet of Grace*. It is a book that I return to again and again and each time find something new that makes me catch my breath in wonder and discover that what I had seen and loved before in it has power once again to renew my spirit. In the following years he published other nonfiction books based on lectures related to theology and preaching: *Wishful Thinking: A Theological ABC* (1973), a book with humorous and charming definitions of theological ideas; *The Faces of Jesus* (1974), in which Buechner's moving text comments on a magnificent collection of artistic depictions of Jesus in painting and sculpture; *Telling the Truth: The Gospel as Tragedy, Comedy, and Fairy Tale* (1977), the published version of the Lyman Beecher Lectures at Yale on preaching; and *Peculiar Treasures: A Biblical Who's Who* (1979), with articles on biblical characters that wake them from the dead for us and wake us from the dead for them. I read them all with joy and with mounting admiration for the breadth and seeming inexhaustibility of Buechner's imagination.

But I have gotten myself ahead of my story or better, perhaps, ahead of his stories. While working on the Noble Lectures, a new character sprang out of a magazine he was reading in a barbershop and took firm hold of whatever in Buechner manufactures his yarns. The name Buechner gave to this character was Leo Bebb. Over the next few years, this mail-order evangelist took over Buechner's fiction, first for one novel, *Lion Country* (1971), and then, refusing to get out of the author's life, for three more—*Open Heart* (1972), *Love Feast* (1974), and *Treasure Hunt* (1977). This tetralogy is the result of his most brilliant surge of creativity to date. I love these novels—the amazing people, the astounding events, and the profound reflection on the human condition in the presence of God and our fellow mortals.

Then, as though responding to a challenge from someone, "You can't possibly top Leo Bebb," Buechner wrote *Godric* (1981). Godric is a roistering, medieval trader and reprobate who, in his forties, finds faith erupting so forcefully in his life that he decides to become a hermit. And then as he lives beyond the hundred-year mark, he finds an uncomfortable sainthood thrust upon him. It has all the Buechner ability to draw us into a storied world, to make us listen to the characters and discover that they are talking directly to us, and to compel us to take even the impossible possibility of God and faith in God with complete seriousness.

With this immersion and involvement in Buechner's writing and having fallen thoroughly under the spell of this multifaceted novelist/ theologian and verbal magician, I was ready and eager for the two volumes of autobiography when they appeared: *The Sacred Journey* (1982) and *Now and Then* (1983). Because his life as an artist is so intricately entwined with his Christian faith, the autobiographical books have all the artistic power of the novels, just as his fiction has throughout the smell of reality and human belief about it. I find that each part of his writing throws light on the other parts. Through all, whether fiction, nonfiction, or autobiography, we glimpse his quest toward wholeness.

And then there is *A Room Called Remember: Uncollected Pieces* (1984). I heard Buechner present three of the "pieces" collected here when he was in Berkeley for the Earl Lectures and Pastoral Conference at Pacific School of Religion in 1983. It was a great time, listening to him speak, having him visit classes to talk about his work, and being given the opportunity in informal settings to become better acquainted with this shy and profound human being.

Included in *A Room Called Remember* are some essays that reveal more about his literary mentors and the sources of his ability to weave his spells of enchantment. I shall return to this book, as well as the others, and give a more complete account of their contents later, with varied perspectives.

For some, the merging of faith and fiction in Buechner's work presents a problem. Amos Wilder, in his review of *The Final Beast*, poses this issue that confronts all who read Buechner—not only those who belong to the Christian community, but also those who identify themselves with other communities of faith. Wilder puts the problem this way:

> In Frederick Buechner's new novel, *The Final Beast* (Atheneum, 1965), we have a good test case of whether a modern artist can make traditional Christian language probable or palatable or effective to a general audience today. Can a novelist or playwright be unashamedly Christian in this sense, naively evangelical; can he deal directly with prayer, miracles, absolution without seeming preachy, without losing the secular reader or even the sophisticated Christian? Can one do it without being typed immediately with certain religious best sellers, which have indeed a large public but not a discriminating one? What the Christian artist can do today, and how he does it, should be revealing for all types of believing witness.[2]

Buechner does indeed provide a superb test case. He writes from within the Christian community of faith and interpretation. He deals with issues in the perspective provided by that community and at times uses words and images that we are more accustomed to hearing in church than from a novelist. But his novels never appear sermonic or liturgical, nor does he project a Christian faith that is pietistic, narrow, or exclusivistic. His honesty, sensitivity, and perception of the ambiguities of life prevent his novels from sounding preachy. His imagination and craft provide him with a wealth of ways to handle religious themes so they emerge in persuasive forms. And his earthy language and realistic situations, which we are not accustomed to hearing about very often in churches, keep him close to the actual world in which his readers live.

What he is doing and the means by which he does it persuade me that Frederick Buechner is one of the most brilliant and distinctive representatives of the Christian movement today. He is a gifted novelist and educated theologian who is able to combine art and faith in ways that are realistic yet fill us with wonder. I find this combination so distinctive that I call Buechner a novelist/theologian. In a time when we desperately need fresh imagination and new language, symbols, and metaphors to express the concerns of Christian faith, an artist of Buechner's depth of sensitivity and creativity has been for me, and indeed for many others, a fantastic find.

Though it is correct to speak of Buechner specifically and gloriously as a person of Christian faith, we must not leap to the conclusion that his is a facile faith, that he arrived at it easily, or that it comes to him again each day without difficulty. There is continually a great deal of turmoil in his believing and no small amount of doubt included in the compound that can be called his Christian faith. There is in him a tremendous longing to believe. Yet the doubt remains starkly underlined in his constant emphasis on the question, Is it true?

In Buechner's faith there is a large *in spite of* that looms around it all. If anyone believes, it is not because it is easy. Rather, one believes in spite of all the strong, sound, convincing reasons for not believing. The theological imagination with which Buechner deals with the ambiguous nature of faith can be seen in many places, but nowhere with greater poignancy than in *The Final Beast*. Here is one example.

The young minister, Nicolet, whose wife had been killed in a senseless auto accident some months previously, takes off on a trip early one morning with no advance warning, leaving his two small girls in the care of the housekeeper, Irma Reinwasser. His brief note gives her no real explanation for his sudden departure. As Irma, a survivor of a Nazi concentration camp, ponders his going, she first asks herself why he would go away like that from home, church, and community. Suddenly the question changes for her to, Why should he stay? She can think of no answer to that question except the children. It couldn't be the church and his ministry, she thinks. That was mainly old ladies, dying and clutching at him, who left him haggard, with knots in his stomach. "The doctor told him that there was nothing wrong with him but just that he had sat out too many terminal cancers—a simple stroke, heart failure, and he would be back on his feet again" (*FB*, 12). Why should he stay?

> There was God, of course, but God made Irma Reinwasser very angry. He asked so much of His servants and rendered so little: marry and bury, christen and counsel, joke with, solicit from, try somehow to live by Him, live with Him. It emptied a man. Yet skinny and bright-eyed in his black robe, he still had to stand up in the pulpit Sunday after Sunday and speak to Him and about Him to that big, white, half-filled meeting-house of a church with the turkey-red carpet, "And when they tell me he looks like Abe Lincoln," Irma said, "I tell them after Abe Lincoln got shot is what he looks like. If you got God for a friend, you don't need any enemies." What did God give in return? A dead wife, knots in the stomach. She plucked up the bacon with a cooking fork and flipped it over. It spat at her. Why should Bluebeard stay for the sake of God? (*FB*, 13)

Faith, for Buechner, has that "in spite of" quality about it, or it has little reality or depth. *The Return of Ansel Gibbs* provides another good example. Henry Kuykendall, who I have mentioned is the character Buechner modeled after his seminary professor James Muilenburg, has given up a professorship at Harvard to become the minister of an East Harlem church that works with people walking dead-end urban streets of poverty and despair. At one point, in a state of great passion, he is speaking to a group of seminarians, "his hands trembling on the heavy leather Bible, his voice now almost inaudibly low, now strident, saying:"

> If anybody starts talking to me about religious commitment, I may listen politely, but what I'd like to answer him with is a few

monosyllables that don't bear repeating here in the midst of the holy community. If you tell me Christian commitment is a thing that has happened to you once and for all like some kind of spiritual plastic surgery, I say go to, go to, you're either pulling the wool over your own eyes or trying to pull it over mine. Every morning you should wake up in your beds and ask yourself: 'Can I believe it all again today?' No, better still, don't ask it till after you've read *The New York Times*, till after you've studied that daily record of the world's brokenness and corruption, which should always stand side by side with your Bible. Then ask yourself if you can believe in the Gospel of Jesus Christ again for that particular day. If your answer's always Yes, then you probably don't know what believing means. At least five times out of ten the answer should be No because the No is as important as the Yes, maybe more so. The No is what proves you're human in case you should ever doubt it. And then if some morning the answer happens to be really Yes, it should be a Yes that's choked with confession and tears and . . . great laughter. Not a beatific smile, but the laughter of wonderful incredulity. (*RAG*, 303–4)

What Kuykendall says in the novel emerges from Buechner's own experience as he has wrestled with his life and faith. One of those crucial events in his life that caught him off guard and made him listen provides a key to the perspective he brings to his writing and also, I am convinced, an important clue to his merging of faith and fiction. This event is what must be called his experience of conversion, if this word is not taken to mean some final, once-for-all happening, but instead a profound change in his life. It happened to him while he was listening to a sermon in the Madison Avenue Presbyterian Church. As we can see, the key element of that experience appears in changed form in Kuykendall's sermon. Buechner writes:

Part of the farce was that for the first time in my life that year in New York, I started going to church regularly, and what was farcical about it was not that I went but my reason for going, which was simply that on the same block where I lived there happened to be a church with a preacher I had heard of and that I had nothing all that much better to do with my lonely Sundays. The preacher was a man named George Buttrick, and Sunday after Sunday I

went, and sermon after sermon I heard. It was not just his eloquence that kept me coming back, though he was wonderfully eloquent, literate, imaginative, never letting you guess what he was
going to come out with next but twitching with surprises up there
in the pulpit. . . . What drew me more was whatever it was that his
sermons came from and whatever it was in me that they touched
so deeply. And then there came one particular sermon with one
particular phrase in it that does not even appear in a transcript of
his words that somebody sent me more than twenty-five years later
so I can only assume that he must have dreamed it up at the last
minute and ad-libbed it—and on just such foolish, tenuous, holy
threads as that, I suppose, hang the destinies of us all. Jesus Christ
refused the crown that Satan offered him in the wilderness, Buttrick said, but he is king nonetheless because again and again he
is crowned in the heart of the people who believe in him. And that
inward coronation takes place, Buttrick said, "among confession,
and tears, and great laughter." (SJ, 108–9)

It sounds like good sermon material to me, and Buttrick, I am told,
was sufficiently magisterial in his delivery as to make even the multipli-
cation table sound holy. It is not, however, what the preacher said that
interests me most, but rather Buechner's *response* to it, a response that
shook him to the core of his being. To get the internal view of what
happened to him, I shall pick up his memory of the experience from
another report he gives:

> It was around the time that Elizabeth II was crowned at West-
> minster Abbey. . . .
> He said that unlike Elizabeth's coronation in the Abbey, this
> coronation of Jesus in the believer's heart took place among
> confession—and I thought, yes, yes, confession—and tears, he
> said—and I thought tears, yes, perfectly plausible that the corona-
> tion of Jesus in the believing heart should take place among confes-
> sion and tears. And then with his head bobbing up and down so
> that his glasses glittered, he said in his odd, sandy voice, the voice
> of an old nurse, that the coronation of Jesus took place among con-
> fession and tears and then, as God was and is my witness, *great
> laughter*, he said. Jesus is crowned among confession and tears and
> great laughter, and at the phrase *great laughter*, for reasons that I

have never satisfactorily understood, the great wall of China crumbled and Atlantis rose up out of the sea, and on Madison Avenue, at 73rd Street, tears leapt from my eyes as though I had been struck across the face. (*AG*, 43–44)

With that shaking of his foundation, Buechner underwent a great turning, an experience of *metanoia*, that has shaped his life decisively since that experience.

The "conversion," however, did not plunge him into a slough of dogmatic rigidities. Instead it was the culmination of a secret seeking in his life and the embarkation upon a further phase of his journey, now shaped by a Christian faith that had about it a delicate, indelible ambiguity. Steeped in commitment as firm as is possible for humans, Buechner's Christian believing retains that honest, open doubt and lack of final knowing that imbues faith with gratitude for having received a great gift. And with the gratitude there comes the awareness of walking into a magnificent mystery. It is this faith that emerges from his conversion, is embodied in his novels, and permeates all his writing.

It is tempting to suggest that Buechner's work as novelist/theologian could be summed up under the headings of confession, tears, laughter. Such a pattern makes considerable sense in theological perspective.

Professor H. Richard Niebuhr, one of the great theologians of this century, says that a continuing peril for Christian theology and ethics is self-defensiveness. He seeks to avoid this error by affirming Christian faith in what he calls confessional ways. The Christian community is called to tell the story of what has happened to us in our history and experience, he says, rather than being called to impose dogmas on others or attempt to prove what other communities believe is false.[3] Buechner as theologian and novelist follows this advice. Faith for him is not abstract and dogmatic but personal and active. He reports events, tells a story, and confesses the trust and meaning that have been given through experience. Witness to his faith in God flows through his writing as what has happened and is happening to him and, in transmuted form, through him to the characters in his fiction. Meaning, in Buechner's view, is in no sense obvious in human life, but it can be discerned if you are looking for it. He never states Christianity as beliefs that everyone must hold in order to be saved. Faith comes instead as a strange and inexplicable gift, appearing in ways just as unexpected and seemingly accidental as his own finding and being found in a church on Madison Avenue.

His stories take place also amid tears. There is bad news as well as good news in the world about which he writes. The Gospel, as a proclamation of the reality in which we believe that we live and move and have our being, tells of tragedy before it gives hope of triumph, offers a message in which suffering encloses the promise. Buechner's characters and plots are drenched in tears. There is, for example, his own father's suicide that he uses so movingly in *The Return of Ansel Gibbs*. Or again, Theodore Nicolet, the preacher in *The Final Beast*, is rescued by the self-sacrifice of his Jewish housekeeper from an attempt to discredit him. In *Lion Country*, Antonio Parr's twin sister is dying of cancer; Leo Bebb has done time in prison; and Lucille Bebb lives out her half-insane existence drowning in alcohol and guilt over her baby's death.

Yet in the midst of the tears, there are still those glimpses of irony, the humorous twists of life, and the sudden bursts of great laughter that throw a different light, like a bolt of lightning, on our suffering, and may sometimes produce those revolutions of perspective that we call conversion. In varied and surprising ways Buechner exhibits in his writing a keen sense of the comic at the heart of faith. Leo Bebb's trick eyelid provides a wink to add an antic touch to the most serious moments. The Joking Cousin performs his function as jester for the strange clan of Indians roaming through *Lion Country* and *Open Heart*.

Perhaps it is the selfsame laughter that in variant form can be found in Francis Thompson's "Hound of Heaven," a "running laughter" beneath which we try unsuccessfully to hide from God. In Buechner's work the humor always lies just under the surface, ready to erupt in illuminating and delightful ways, as likely to reveal as to conceal God's presence in unexpected places and to show us who and where we really are.

The laughter, sometimes quiet, sometimes explosive, that Buechner brings to his writing might be likened also to the laughter of God in Psalm 2, where God laughs in derision at those with earthly dominion who attempt to set themselves against God's purposes. In the psalm the divine laughter is both judgmental and cleansing; it places all human claims in eternal perspective.

And Buechner too is not just playing for laughs but is drawing his readers to think beyond the laughter to the irony it suggests and to the insights such laughter can bring. With humor Buechner provides an angle of vision on life too often lacking in contemporary religion. He compels us to laugh at what we might otherwise take to be real and, through laughter, prods us to find ourselves confronted with an alternative vision filled with the possibilities of healing. Or, to say it another way: because religious faith always runs the risk of taking itself too seriously, in sermons or religious literature, we may focus too easily on some ideal of God or ourselves and forget our humanity. Humor reminds us of the ridiculous aspect of our pretensions in daring to speak of God at all and keeps us aware that all faith is a precarious balance between what is all too real and what is completely impossible; between the creation-wide mercy of God as Christians affirm it and the self-centered, sectarian pettiness of human religion. Buechner reminds us that laughter can help us make sense out of the experience of believers, caught between guilty sainthood and holy charlatanry. Humor for Buechner becomes an ironic instrument for affirming our fallen yet grace-filled lives, a kind of artistic thermometer for taking our temperature as we reach longingly toward spiritual health and wholeness.

In a discussion with students in my class when he was in Berkeley, Buechner remarked, "Whether it is my blessing or my curse, my style is antic." And just to remind us of the laughter at the center of Christian faith, he writes about doubt as follows:

> Whether your faith is that there is a God or that there is not a God, if you don't have any doubts you are either kidding yourself or asleep.
> Doubts are the ants in the pants of faith. They keep it awake and moving. (*WT*, 20)

I admitted earlier that I was tempted to speak of Buechner's work as contained within the triad of confession, tears, and laughter, and to some extent I have yielded. But though these three permeate his faith and fiction, they do not do full justice to the artistry present in all he writes. The aura of fairy tale surrounds his stories, a wistful air of wishful imagination, yet his characters, events, and action seem drawn from genuine human experiences, painfully and hopefully and ludicrously real. This interweaving of fantasy and actuality gives his novels an overpowering sense of fitting our human experience more adequately than various realisms or sheer fairy tale could accomplish alone. How he pulls his rabbits from some unlikely hats is, I believe, the key to Buechner's magical achievement. Though it will be possible only to a limited extent, I shall try my best to show how he learned to perform his literary tricks and how he works his sleight of hand for the holy ends of a novelist/theologian.

Looked at together, what Buechner has written adds up to a sizable body of literature. In looking at his work from different directions, I shall include all the books he has published so far. As there are many people who read his fiction but not his nonfiction and vice versa, it may prove helpful to see the continuities that run throughout his work. And, of course, those who have read little of Buechner will find here an introduction to his total work as represented in his major publications to date.

In my view, Buechner is doing a distinctively new thing on the literary scene, writing novels that are theologically exciting without becoming propaganda, and doing theology with artistic style and imagination. Until recently, theology has been limited almost completely to dry, logical, and inartistic discussions of a series of standard topics such as God, Revelation, the Bible, Creator, Jesus Christ, Holy Spirit, and so on. Biblical scholarship has usually been preoccupied with linguistic, historical, and textual matters, as though what is collected in the Jewish–Christian Scriptures has little or no relation to the traditions and communities of human believing that assembled, validated, preserved, and continue to make use of these writings in worship and as wellsprings of faith and action.

And novelists often write as though they are unaware of any religious dimensions of believed-in reality shaping the world delineated in the enveloping action of their work. From reading most contemporary fiction, it would appear that many human beings go neither to church nor to the toilet, neither believe in God nor defecate. With notable exceptions, the convictions and commitments embodied in the story are not explored in terms of their theological horizons. The impression often left is that the authors are not even aware of the extent to which their own apparent theology gives to the authors themselves the place of deity.

In an era when the narrative form of theology is being recovered and the Bible is being seen afresh as the Scriptures of living traditions, Buechner stands out sharply as a profoundly innovative pioneer of faith. In the careful crafting of his stories in their religious dimensions, he is also doing a new thing in the writing of novels. Although he cannot point this creative combination out about himself, I can do it.

As you read these pages, it will become apparent that it is not my intention to present a literary critique of Buechner's work. Rather, I want to share what I have discovered in his books: a perception of life and faith that illumines my own in fascinating and wonderful ways and may do the same for you.

Buechner speaks of himself at times as an "evangelist" or an "apologist" who is trying to speak of "the possibility of God."[4] Perhaps it is most accurate to say that I see myself as an evangelist or apologist for Frederick Buechner. That does not mean that I want to be a publicist for him. Instead, I want to draw others into the experience of discovery and deep appreciation that has been mine in reading him. I wish for others that experience of secondary creativity which Tillich defines and which I have felt myself as I have read Buechner's writing. Of this secondary creativity, Tillich writes:

> In order to be spiritually creative one need not be what is called a creative artist or scientist or statesman, but one must be able to participate meaningfully in their original creations. Such a participation is creative insofar as it changes that in which one participates, even if in very small ways. The creative transformation of a language by the interdependence of the creative poet or writer and the many who are influenced by him directly or indirectly and react spontaneously to him is an outstanding example. Everyone who lives creatively in meanings affirms himself as a participant in these meanings. He affirms himself as receiving and transforming reality creatively. He loves himself as participating in the spiritual life and as loving its contents. He loves them because they are his own fulfillment and because they are actualized through him.[5]

In this sense I want to draw attention to Buechner's artistic insight and accomplishment so that others will read his books, participate in his creativity, and find for themselves a way into what he calls "the holy and hidden heart of life."

Who are those others likely to be? Who are the people who may become Buechner's audience? For whom does he write? Drawing on his years as preacher and teacher at Exeter, he has said that he hopes he writes to the Exeter boy in all of us. He thinks that the concerns and fears, hopes and desires, thoughts and aspirations, of these students are essentially those shared by all persons as they trace out their own journeys of faith and life. Preposterous as it sounds, Buechner may be correct, correct in what he perceives humans to be concerned about, and at least correct enough to find his audience growing in numbers and in attachment to his characters and the insights they invite us to discover about ourselves.

Because of the moral complexity of the human situation as he presents it and the ironic turns his writing takes, Buechner suspects that his books are "too religious for secular readers," and "too secular for religious ones" (NT, 108). Remarking on this possibility, Amos Wilder says that "the Christian presence in the novel or the pulpit today works like a sieve or a crucible and continually selects out a new people as in all times." Thus, those of us who have become more alive through reading Buechner are those "new people." Our number appears to be growing all the time!

Reading any of Buechner's varied works will, I believe, be provocative for all those who struggle with the difficulties of understanding and expressing the faith by which they live. But his work can be especially helpful for Christians in relation to their own experiences and their own styles of believing and living. By using story and parable, tears and laughter, realism and fairy tale, characters who embody the ambiguity of us all, and themes that reflect the human issues of living and dying, Buechner stimulates his readers to delve more deeply into the meaning of their own experience and discover anew its dimensions of faith.

Trying to understand him at a distance is not enough, not even through my own response to him in this book. People must read, hear, and encounter Buechner himself and the characters he creates, and absorb what they discover from it all into their own lives. If my own experience of him leads others to read him, as Amos Wilder's review did for me, these pages will have fulfilled the hopes I have had as I wrote them.

His writing is neither "too religious" nor "too secular" for a growing host of us. Indeed, he helps us see that these terms are often misleading. For Buechner, the most ordinary as well as the extraordinary events of human life bear sacredness and grace within them. And both creation and redemption in God's covenant reach out and embrace the whole world. In this book I hope to illustrate and interpret Buechner's understanding of the wholeness and the holiness of all human experience, which comes to us "among confession, and tears, and great laughter."

CHAPTER 1

A New Creation:
Art and Theology in Covenant

"We all got secrets. I got them same as everybody else—things we feel bad about and wish hadn't ever happened. Hurtful things. Long ago things." Leo Bebb, the diploma-mill evangelist, is talking at the big Thanksgiving dinner in *Love Feast*. He has plenty of secrets, as we discover in Buechner's novels about him, but he also has a knack for bringing life and healing. "We're all scared and lonesome," he says at the dinner, "but most of the time we keep it hid. It's like every one of us has lost his way so bad we don't even know which way is home any more only we're ashamed to ask. You know what would happen if we would own up we're lost and ask? Why, what would happen is we'd find out home is each other. We'd find out home is Jesus that loves us lost or found or any whichway" (*LF* in *BB*, 306–7).

As novelist/theologian of the lost and found, Frederick Buechner has a depth and sensitivity encountered all too seldom. He knows how to tell a story, tell it well, and tell it so that it moves from the experienced surface of our lives into the most significant recesses of existence. In so doing, he discloses himself to be not only an artist of astonishing gifts and growing stature, but also a religious thinker of profound insight and powerful expression. His theological writing is shaped by his ability as storyteller, and his fiction is permeated by an informed theological perspective. With great artistry he draws us into his stories, probing the human spirit at the deepest levels of faith.

"Art does not reproduce what we see," says Paul Klee, the Swiss painter. "It makes us see." Buechner is doing just that: making us see. As we are pulled into the flow of his imagination, something important and different happens to us. What happens is important because he speaks to us so that we see more clearly who we are and begin to get glimpses of a reality in which we live and move and have our being. What happens to us is different in that we are not merely watching a story unfold like reels of a movie but becoming ourselves part of the drama so that we see differently and may even be transformed. What Buechner does is so important, different, and innovative that I call it a new creation. I shall try to explain what I mean by that phrase and in the process show the fascinating interweaving of faith and fiction that Buechner achieves.

Within the reality of the world as we experience it, artistry and faith can be distinguished but not separated. They are so intimately and intricately intertwined in human life as to make it impossible to say with precision and certainty where one leaves off and the other begins.

The inseparability of faith and art stands out with special clarity in the ongoing life of the world's great religious traditions. The scriptures that embody the basic teachings of these traditions differ widely, but have a central area of similarity in that the ultimate commitments to which believers are called are expressed in stories and historical narratives having artistic form and power. Like the tale told by Coleridge's ancient mariner, these narratives have a compelling quality given them by their combination of faith and art.

In the Christian tradition most theology is heavily rationalistic and usually devoid of art, but this is not the case with the Christian Bible and the devotional writings and hymns that down through the centuries have borne and depicted the impulses toward God forming the core of that religious tradition. Theologians, it would appear, are more intent on imitating the style of philosophers such as Aristotle or Hegel than on modeling their work on writings that have emerged from and nurtured the call of God to faith. The philosopher Alfred North Whitehead reminds us that "religions commit suicide when they find their inspiration in their dogmas. The inspiration of religion lies in the history of religion."[6]

Buechner is a theologian who uses the novel and personal narrative to express the puzzles and mysteries of faith. As such, he is contributing to the recovery of vital Christian expression. In him a lost dimension of faith is being found.

Though it is often not so obvious even to artists or their publics, art inescapably has dimensions of believing and valuing that are expressed more directly in religious faith. These dimensions of faith — specifically

Christian faith—are readily apparent in such works as Dante's *Divine Comedy*, Milton's *Paradise Lost*, and Eliot's *Four Quartets*. Hermann Hesse's *Glasperlenspiel*, as well as his other novels, exhibits dimensions of faith, more Eastern than Western. Thorton Wilder probes the meaning of faith, in, for example, *The Bridge of San Luis Rey* with great artistic sensitivity. Although sharing the commitments of the Christian community, Wilder does not see them clearly confirmed in human experience. He sees only in bits and pieces, not with wholeness, yet he can affirm, "There is a land of the living and a land of the dead and the bridge is love, the only survival, the only meaning."

Like Milton, Eliot, and Wilder, Buechner is clear that his own faith is Christian rather than some other, as with Hesse. But he is less certain than Milton and Eliot that human experience unquestionably confirms what Christians believe. More like Wilder in perceiving the ambiguity, the bits and pieces the world presents to us, he nevertheless goes further than Wilder in affirming meaning, Christian meaning, as a possibility hidden within our experience if we are looking for it, as a truth too good not to be true, as a cosmic joke too funny for mere words if we have enough sense of humor to catch it.

In this perspective we can understand Buechner best if we see him performing a fascinating juggling act, with art embodying faith in a tantalizing way that never lets us evade responsibility for our own believing. In his combination of the two, faith is that comprehensive meaning that can best be pointed to through art.

For Buechner, art and faith are involved in the whole of our experience and especially in what we believe about creation and history. The very notion of creation requires delving behind experience into its roots and its possibility in ways that require artistic forms to convey our meaning. And this meaning will inevitably exhibit theological overtones. He writes:

> When God created the Creation he made something where before there had been nothing, and as the author of The Book of Job puts it, "the morning stars sang together, and all the sons of God shouted for joy" (Job 38:7) at the sheer and shimmering novelty of the thing. "New every morning is the love / Our wakening and uprising prove" says the hymn. Using the same old materials of earth, air, fire, and water, every twenty-four hours God creates something new out of them. If you think you're seeing the same

show all over again seven times a week, you're crazy. Every morning you wake up to something that in all eternity never was before and never will be again. And the you that wakes up was never the same before and will never be the same again either. (*WT*, 18)

In the same way, a person's view of history also exhibits theological overtones and undertones:

> Unlike Buddhism or Hinduism, biblical faith takes history very seriously because God takes it very seriously. . . . The biblical view is that history is not an absurdity to be endured or an illusion to be dispelled or an endlessly repeating cycle to be escaped. Instead it is for each of us a series of crucial, precious, and unrepeatable moments that are seeking to lead us somewhere.
> . . . True history has to do with the saving and losing of souls, and both of these are apt to take place when most people including the one whose soul is at stake are looking the other way. (*WT*, 38)

History as salvation brings meaning to us, gives us a sense of an enveloping action or theological story that is unfolding in the past, present, and future as we experience them. With the insight given in faith, historical meaning extends beyond particular events and suggests the relation among happenings. Image and story can then serve as a vehicle by which the overall pattern of meaning comes into view. Faith and art, for Buechner, come together in mutual dependence. They are bound together and are inseparable. Such close, symbiotic relation can be characterized most accurately as a covenant.

Covenantal relationships are familiar to those whose religious faith has been shaped by the biblical tradition. There we discover that the world of nature and history, of which we are a part, has been created within the faithful unity of God's covenant with us. The world has, therefore, a wholeness and interconnectedness. No event in our lives, or in the created order, is unrelated to everything and everyone else. Every occurrence has significance within the attention of God. As we discern relations and interconnections among particular events and circumstances of ordinary experience, meaning emerges for us. The covenanted significance of creation, as God communicates it to us, comes incarnationally, that is, embodied within events, relationships, and persons. It is in our thoughts and in our interactions with people and nature that God is revealed to us, that our redemption comes, and through which we work out our individual and societal destinies.

It may seem strange at first to speak of art and theology in covenant, but Buechner's writing makes it believable. He takes the fragments of experience and discloses them, if we want to see, as pointing to the network of relations, loyalties, and commitments making up the fabric of our lives. Then we recognize that only in artistic ways can that wholeness of living, with its depth of faith, be expressed. Art becomes a form of theology, and theology emerges as a way to understand the deepest and most encompassing meaning of a work of art. With art and theology so inseparably and inescapably woven into the depth of human experience, nothing less than a notion such as covenant seems adequate to express their relationship or to convey the way they are bound together in Buechner's writing.

In the review I mention in the previous chapter, Amos Wilder points to the artistic integration of faith and life that Buechner achieves in *The Final Beast:*

> Here he writes as a Christian using Christian themes and doctrines explicitly. Yet this is no liturgical fable for the sanctuary alone. The evangelical formulas and behavior are located unmistakably in the midst of the world's business and obsessions. The devout reader may even be shocked by the worldliness of the setting and language. We have an uncompromising Christian witness in the narration; yet it makes a bold bid to be receivable, palatable and convincing to the disabused agnostic—precisely because the author offers equal credentials of sophistication along with his artistic mastery.[7]

In the past, more often than not, art and theology have been treated, especially by academics, as separate spheres or disciplines, with completely different ways of perceiving life. At times it would appear in the view of some that the two are not related at all or only incidentally so because art occasionally has religious themes.

When I say that Frederick Buechner is doing something new, I am speaking of the way he understands and illustrates that art and theology are in covenant. This is Buechner's "new creation." Art and theology are full and equal partners in our human quest for meaning and in our ceaseless attempts to articulate the meaning we discern in our experience. Theology as storytelling about what we believe to be real merges into fiction as the artistic presentation of experience reaches toward meaning. In the perspective of Buechner's new creation, the bond between art and theology is necessary and complete.

In all that follows I shall be explaining what I understand Buechner's new creation means in his writing, what it means in his own life, and how, as it speaks to us, it can bring life to our old, faded meanings.

In Buechner's work the covenanted interrelation of art and theology has many facets. The interdependence between the two can be seen most clearly as he tells us and then demonstrates how story can become parable, how art incarnates one or another believed-in reality, and how, through parable and incarnated meaning, theology at the height of its expression is metaphor.

STORY AS PARABLE

How do you invite people to a parable, Antonio Parr wonders in *Love Feast* (*LF* in *BB*, 303). Well, Frederick Buechner seems to have found some deliciously attractive ways to do it in our time, just as Jesus did in his.

"A parable," Buechner says, "is a small story with a large point." Jesus told stories about ordinary people and events. Yet those stories were intended to convey meanings beyond the ordinary. Indeed, the significance they bear becomes extraordinary. "Most of the ones Jesus told," Buechner continues,

> have a kind of sad fun about them. The parables of the Crooked Judge (Luke 18:1–8), the Sleepy Friend (Luke 11:5–8), and the Distraught Father (Luke 11:11–13) are really jokes in their way, at least part of whose point seems to be that a silly question deserves a silly answer. In the Prodigal Son (Luke 15:11–32) the elder brother's pious pique when the returning prodigal gets the red-carpet treatment is worthy of Moliere's *Tartuffe*, as is the outraged legalism of the Laborers in the Vineyard (Matthew 20:1–16) when Johnny-Come-Lately gets as big a slice of the worm as the Early Bird. The point of the Unjust Steward is that it's better to be a resourceful rascal than a saintly schlemiel (Luke 16:1–8), and of the Talents that, spiritually speaking, playing the market will get you further than playing it safe (Matthew 25:14–30). (*WT*, 66–67)

Buechner picks up on the sad fun of Jesus' parables in his own stories. And they become parables because they convey a larger point. I think of the parable of the Talents when Leo Bebb says of his assistant, Laverne Brown: "Now, you take a man like Brownie, Antonio, and you ask yourself where the Almighty went wrong. Well, I tell you it's not the Almighty went wrong, it's Brownie went wrong. The Almighty gave Brownie life, and Brownie never lived it. He just shoved it up his ass" (*LC* in *BB*, 94). Before you know it, you are thinking of all the people you have met who fit Jesus' parable of the Talents in Buechner's use of it.

The more I read Buechner, the more I appreciate the larger dimensions of stories I run across elsewhere. Here is an illustration of contemporary parable that a friend builds on someone else's real experience.

Loren Eiseley tells a story which helps me feel the power of recognizing life's contradictions. That great naturalist once spent time in a seaside town called Costabel and, plagued by his lifelong insomnia, spent the early morning hours walking the beach. Each day at sunrise he found townspeople combing the sand for starfish which had washed ashore during the night, to kill them for commercial purposes. It was, for Eiseley, a sign, however small, of all the ways the world says no to life.

But one morning Eiseley got up unusually early, and discovered a solitary figure on the beach. This man, too, was gathering starfish, but each time he found one alive he would pick it up and throw it as far as he could out beyond the breaking surf, back to the nurturing ocean from which it came. As the days went by Eiseley found this man embarked on his mission of mercy each morning, seven days a week, no matter the weather.

Eiseley named this man "the star thrower," and in a moving meditation he writes of how this man and his predawn work contradicted everything that Eiseley had been taught about evolution and the survival of the fittest. Here on the beach in Costabel the strong reached down to save, not crush, the weak. And Eiseley wonders: Is there a star thrower at work in the universe, a God who contradicts death, a God whose nature (in the words of Thomas Merton) is "mercy within mercy within mercy"?[8]

This story tugs at my heart, makes a lump come to my throat, and brings tears to my eyes, just as Buechner's tales can do for me. It is a little story with a very large meaning. It is a story become parable.

In Buechner's hands, a parable can also be a big story with an even bigger point. It can be embodied in a novel. In *Godric*, for example, Buechner tells the story of a medieval saint from his perspective as a hundred-year-old man looking back over his long life and forward to his approaching death. Buechner writes that "more than half without knowing it, I was trying on various ways of growing old and facing death myself" (*NT*, 107). The story became a parable that he was telling to himself.

Or again, *The Entrance to Porlock* is a different kind of example. In this book Buechner builds his story around another story. He retells the "parable" of the Wizard of Oz.

Love Feast, the third novel of the Bebb foursome, is also based on another story, this time a parable of Jesus'. It is a modern day elaboration of the parable of the Great Feast. And just possibly, Buechner was gearing up for the writing of that novel when he said of parables:

> Both the sadness and the fun are at their richest, however, in the parable of the Great Banquet (Luke 14:16–24). The Beautiful People all send in their excuses, of course — their real estate, their livestock, their sex lives — so the host sends his social secretary out into the streets to bring in the poor, the maimed, the blind, the lame.
>
> The string ensemble strikes up the overture to *The Bartered Bride*, the champagne glasses are filled, the cold pheasant is passed round, and there they sit by candlelight with their white canes and their empty sleeves, their Youngstown haircuts, their orthopedic shoes, their sleazy clothes, their aluminum walkers. A woman with a harelip proposes a toast. An old man with the face of Lear on the heath and a party hat does his best to rise to his feet. A deaf-mute thinks people are starting to go home and pushes back from the table. Rose petals float in the finger bowls. The strings shift into the *Liebestod*.
>
> With parables and jokes both, if you've got to have it explained, don't bother. (*WT*, 67)

All good writers are undoubtedly aware of the ways that the stories they tell have wider applicability, even though they focus on individuals and on distinctive happenings. Buechner, however, is among that special group of artists who handles the particular with full consciousness of its levels of meaning, extending in his case explicitly to the encompassing level of theological worldview. Like the story of the Good Samaritan, Buechner's novels, understood as parables, draw us into the world he creates, lead us to dwell in that world, and invite us to undergo a revolution of faith and living as a consequence.

My friend Herman Waetjen, a New Testament scholar, taught me that *parable* derives from words meaning "alongside of" and "to cast or throw." Thus Jesus took a story and cast it alongside human experience to heighten our awareness of God's presence among us. There is no better way to read Buechner's fiction than to view it as a series of stories thrown alongside contemporary experience to illumine for us the wonder and mystery of our lives.

Buechner's stories as parables resemble Jesus' in another way: they open us toward a transformed future. "Go, and do likewise," Jesus sometimes says. But the parables direct us toward the future even if these words are not present. The parables of Jesus' are like the stories Plato tells in his *Dialogues* in this respect. Plato's way of resorting to story for the most inclusive levels of reality reminds us that we must remain open with reference to the precision of our knowing and to the possibilities of the future. The story of the ring of Gyges suggests the social nature of ethics, and the myth of the cave discloses the pain, responsibility, and liberating potential of knowledge. Indeed, the dramatic dialogues embody in their inconclusiveness the open-endedness of stories with tremendous points.

Buechner introduces the element of open-endedness in his own distinctive ways. For example, it was in the book barn that Peter Ringkoping had seen ghosts, "if he had seen them at all" (*EP*, 6). Things happen, or do not happen. There is meaning there if you are looking for meaning. With Plato and Jesus, Buechner invites us to the openness of knowing and believing.

As I have enjoyed the stories Buechner tells and watched them turn into parables, or seen him take parables and use them as the bases of stories, it has occurred to me that story as parable points us toward art as incarnation and theology as metaphor. This sequence starts us on the way toward seeing Buechner as novelist and theologian. Storytelling for him is the process of making action and language incarnate. And the way that the writer's art incarnates believed-in reality is through parable in the form of well-told stories that convey larger messages.

ART AS INCARNATION

In the foreword to *Theology and Modern Literature,* Amos Wilder says, "I recognize that a work of art is first of all and always to be understood in its own aesthetic terms." He is convinced that the autonomy of art must be provided with safeguards in order to shield it from alien pressures. But critics, he suggests, may be so protective of art as to overlook or deny the encompassing dimensions of meaning a work of art embodies. "I believe," he continues, "that all imaginative creations from the oldest myth and ritual to the most recent poem have their own kind of declarative or cognitive role, offer 'news of reality.'"[9]

Any attempt to separate the being from the meaning of a poem, or any work of art, is based on a false dichotomy. Artistic creation cannot be reduced to the dogmas either of the theologian or the critic. But there are inescapable dimensions of meaning in the being of art. To deny them is no less a reductive attack on the autonomy of art than attempts to turn it into concepts or propaganda.

Buechner avoids both horns of this supposed dilemma. With Wilder, he understands art as incarnational. By this they intend to say that meaning must be embodied in actions, words, or artifacts, and that these embodiments actually or potentially convey meaning. He writes:

> Words written fifty years ago, a hundred years ago, a thousand years ago, can have as much of this power today as ever they had it then to come alive for us and in us and to make us more alive within ourselves. That, I suppose, is the final mystery as well as the final power of words: that not even across great distances of time and space do they ever lose their capacity for becoming incarnate. And when these words tell of virtue and nobility, when they move us closer to that truth and gentleness of spirit by which we become fully human, the reading of them is sacramental; and a library is as holy a place as any temple is holy because through the words which are treasured in it the Word itself becomes flesh again and again and dwells among us and within us, full of grace and truth. (*RCR,* 181)

We note also in a passage such as this that Buechner adds his own distinctive twist. What he says is not dogma but confession of his own faith. This confessional element must be kept in mind, he believes, lest we forget that faith remains in part mystery, and that we who receive its gift remain faulted, fallible beings. "Because the word that God speaks to us," he writes, "is always an incarnate word—a word spelled out to us not alphabetically, in syllables, but enigmatically, in events, even in the books we read and the movies we see—the chances are we will never get it just right" (NT, 3).

In this sentence Buechner is not merely making an observation. He is suggesting the way he understands the relation between theology and art. Because the incarnational character of God's speaking involves considerable ambiguity, Buechner emphasizes, it is highly unlikely that we will be able to interpret and communicate it completely or with final certainty.

All works of art are attempts to embody and make visible some feeling or perception of the artist. In their artistic endeavors, I believe, artists reach for the holy and divine task of creation, and their spirits may pervade their works even as God's spirit pervades the creation and was incarnate in Jesus Christ.

Buechner is acutely aware of this ongoing process of art as incarnational on many levels. On one level we incarnate our faith, in conscious and unconscious ways, by acting out what we believe. What we believe about God is in this way always embodied in the lives of persons and communities. That is, I am convinced, what Buechner means when he says that art is always an incarnate word.

On another level, the word addressed to us by God is, as Buechner sees it, spelled out, not in dramatic and unusual events, but in the ordinary happenings of our life experience. "I am thinking of incarnation," he says, "breath becoming speech through teeth and tongue, spirit becoming word, silence becoming prayer, the holy dream becoming the holy face. I am speaking of the humdrum events of our lives as an alphabet" (AG, 11). It is this alphabet of the ordinary that comes together into the words of meaning that we hear as God's speaking to us. Thus our own lives provide the raw material of our theology. "One of the blunders religious people are particularly fond of making," he perceptively remarks elsewhere, "is the attempt to be more spiritual than God" (WT, 43).

On a still deeper level, artists such as Buechner through their work enable us to experience theological insights in the forms of words, events, and metaphors so that we *see* in ways that were impossible before. The artist turns the opaqueness of our ordinary experience into a glass of vision so we can experience meaning.

Incarnation is an underlying theme in all Buechner's work, as insight into ourselves, our companions, and God emerges in unexpected places. In *Lion Country,* Antonio's first meeting with Lucille, Leo Bebb's wife, illustrates incarnational surprise:

> It had never occurred to me that Bebb might be married. Perhaps it was because of some lingering childhood image of the priesthood that had come loose in my subconscious and attached itself to him—the priest as celibate with the Church his only bride and all men his children. Or perhaps it was because the one time I had seen him in the city he had seemed so much on his own, so sure of himself and in charge, that it never crossed my mind he might have a wife who knew all his tricks by heart, somebody he went away from and came back to and maybe even depended on. . . . I was not prepared even for the idea of a Mrs. Bebb, let alone for its incarnation in Lucille. (*LC* in *BB,* 39)

Artistic creations have the capacity not only to embody dimensions of meaning but also the power to draw us into a deeper level of involvement with the believed-in reality the work of art embodies. When we fall under the spell of art, we experience bursts of insights about ourselves and our world. I describe such times as "dwelling in and breaking out."

For this notion I am indebted to Michael Polanyi. In *Personal Knowledge*[10] he shows that we apprehend reality through various frameworks of interpretation given us by the sociocultural context in which we live. Attempts to hold tightly to received views of reality and claim them as final answers, however, lead toward stagnation, dogmatism, and loss of meaning. When we *dwell in* our convictions about the world with passion—neither merely observing from a distance nor seeking total control, but rather living in them (as we dwell in our bodies)—it becomes possible for new insight to occur, for innovative revelation to happen, for the Buddhist satori to come upon us, for us to have an "aha!" experience. In those times we *break out* of the framework in which we have been dwelling (as we might break out of a prison) to new discovery. It is only by *dwelling in* that *breaking out* becomes possible.

In this perspective we can see how art as incarnation makes it possible to move beyond viewing the artistic creation at a distance and become drawn into its world in ways that lead to a new creation taking shape within us. By entering the world of a work of art, no matter how lighthearted or profound its intent, I believe it is possible for us to gain awareness of our own worlds and emerge with greater insight into ourselves and our relationships.

Most often it is difficult to achieve new vision amid the ordinariness of our lives. Life crowds in upon us; we do not see the implications of our relations or our choices nor understand what other persons experience. Into this human situation art can come as a prophetic and healing experience.

Buechner has the capacity to look at the ordinary that surrounds us and help us to see it incarnating wider realms of meaning with religious faith at the core. He writes:

> Moses at the burning bush was told to take off his shoes because the ground on which he stood was holy ground (Exodus 3:5), and incarnation means that all ground is holy ground because God not only made it but walked on it, ate and slept and worked and died on it. If we are saved anywhere, we are saved here. And what is saved is not some diaphanous distillation of our bodies and our earth but our bodies and our earth themselves. (*WT,* 43)

My own artistic perspective derives especially from my long involvement with drama, the art of acting, of bringing life to life, person to person. The actors dwell in the roles and events of a play and draw the audience into that world. In the process both actor and audience may break out into a new and wider vision. Buechner has this dramatic gift of bringing life to us in his stories so that we dwell in his characters and often break out into deeper insight about ourselves. This is illustrated in the marvelously vivid yet delicate account of Antonio's first sexual experience with Sharon, Bebb's daughter. Bebb has just taken them on a trip to an open-air zoo called Lion Country and then suggested that Antonio take Sharon out to dinner. When the two of them stop by Antonio's motel room to pick up his car keys, he starts questioning her to get information about Bebb for the exposé he intends to write about the mail-order evangelist. After their conversation on this subject, she surprises him by saying, "'Would you be shocked if I asked to wash the lion off here in your shower bath? . . .' Looking back on it, I suspect we both knew what hung on my answer— not that I could have really answered anything other than of course the shower was all hers if she wanted it" (*LC* in *BB*, 74). And then:

> I remember how after a while she was standing there by the bed with the towel wrapped around her like a sarong and holding her damp hair in a pile on top of her head and asking me if I knew where something was, though I haven't the faintest idea what she was asking for and hadn't the faintest idea then. I remember her face was wet still, and there were drops of water caught in her eyelashes. And I remember how far away and almost detached I felt as I reached up with one hand and touched the place just below her shoulder where she had the towel tucked in on itself and how at my touch the towel didn't fall straight to the floor as you might suppose but sideways instead and quite slowly, catching for a moment on the way down.
>
> If I forget thee, let my right hand forget her cunning. If I do not remember thee, let my tongue cleave to the roof of my mouth. I remember that Sharon—that dime-store name—frowned, did she? or smiled her young thief's smile as she raised one hand to her shoulder where my hand had touched, and stepped free from the towel at her feet. (*LC* in *BB*, 75)

Antonio, who has come to Florida to expose Bebb, is himself exposed along with Sharon. And we may perhaps realize that we all are in the end exposed before God and each other.

The insight of new discovery, dwelling in and breaking out, is the meaning of art as incarnation and represents an impulse at the very heart of creation. It is a process involving action and conflict and deep emotion—powerful, exciting, risky—a movement by which new life comes from the death of the old. Buechner lives this process, understands it, and exhibits it in his own new creation.

THEOLOGY AS METAPHOR

To some scholarly practitioners of theology, my designation of

Buechner as a theologian may come as a shock, a shock that deepens as these academics discover the influences on Buechner as a theologian to be not only Paul Tillich but also the Lone Ranger, not only James Muilenburg but also the Oz books. But then, Amos, Jeremiah, and Jesus would certainly be puzzled and possibly even pained by what academic theologians of the Western intellectual tradition have done with the accounts of God in the Jewish and Christian Scriptures.

To the extent that theology can be said to be present in the Bible, it takes varied forms — story, parable, historical narrative, legal code, prophetic utterance, personal address (in letters and preaching), and poetry, to name the most prominent. Permeating all these forms in which faith in God is expressed, and providing their theological depth, is what in literary and artistic perspective is called metaphor. As Buechner incarnates metaphors in his stories that function as parables, the metaphors assume theological dimensions. We may say that Buechner creates artistic expressions that represent Christian theology in metaphorical guise.

Susanne K. Langer says: "The principle of metaphor is simply the principle of saying one thing and meaning another, and expecting to be understood to mean the other."[11] A metaphor may place two images alongside one another so that they throw unexpected light on each other, or a metaphor may describe something unknown with an image of something known. In both ways, a story used as a parable may have metaphorical overtones. When we describe something by referring to it with an idea or name not usually associated with it, we are making use of metaphor.

In the first meaning of metaphor, Buechner speaks of lions "with their narrow hips and hairy, sunflower heads" (*LF* in *BB*, 340). He refers to sunflowers but is really talking about lions' heads, and we know it. And further, we will never look again either at the head of a lion or at a sunflower without thinking of the other. Each image helps us visualize the other more vividly.

In the second sense, a metaphor may be used to describe the indescribable. For example, because human experience of God is indirect rather than direct, something like metaphor or its little sister, simile, must be used to speak of the divine. God is spoken about with word-pictures drawn from ordinary experience that take on extraordinary meaning in this usage. Metaphor in Langer's sense, therefore, is necessary for language about religious experience. It is appropriate that the language of the Bible be metaphorical in order to convey its theological message.

In Buechner's writing, metaphors seem to appear as regularly and as easily as verbs. His novels are permeated by metaphorical expression. As we shall see later in Chapter 6, he affirms that literature by its very nature *is* metaphor. Here, however, we are concerned with the way theology in his writing is expressed through metaphor.

Buechner's interest in metaphorical expression arose prior to his study of the Bible. It began, at least in a focused way, in his fascination with words and literature as a student at Princeton. He wrote his senior thesis as an undergraduate on the function of metaphor in English poetry. At Union Theological Seminary, Paul Tillich showed him the importance of metaphor in theology and the biblical way of using language to express faith in God. Of Tillich's ideas on this subject, Buechner writes:

> I remember his view that any language you apply to God, no matter how apparently straightforward, is actually metaphorical language so that even the words *God exists* cannot be taken literally but only as a kind of poem. God does not stand out of being (*ex* + *sistere*) like the rest of us but is that out of which the possibility of being comes, or the ground of being, to clarify one metaphor by way of another. (*NT*, 14)

Here is a way to put it that has helped me. We cannot expect to discover God in the same sequence of experiences that we have of rocks, chairs, bodies, television sets, space shuttles, and planets. But then, neither are life, development, embarrassment, neuroses, commitment, pain, or love to be found in the same way as doors, feet, or water. That does not mean that embarrassment or pain, for example, are any less real than the ground on which we are standing or the beds in which we sleep. Life and love are embodied as we experience them in things, and things do not occur apart from human experience, interpretation, and validation. God, as the believed-in reality providing the basis of value and validity and the ground of being for everything that exists—things, feelings, meaning—is the most encompassing level of human experiencing. These levels of experience are inseparable. We never have a choice between body and mind, between things and ideas, between facts and faith. They come together in symbiotic bonding, distinguishable but present to us only in a covenant of interdependence. Buechner understands this covenanted unity of human experience and recognizes that metaphor, combining literary and theological perspectives, is necessary to express the holy wholeness that is God.

His use of metaphor shows the inseparable bond between art and theology through vivid images drawn from experience and set within stories that illumine faith. On the one hand, his artistic way of doing theology has distinctive biblical qualities about it. And on the other hand, the rich Technicolor of the metaphors that communicate his theology resonate in our own experience because they have been lifted out of the depth of his. Rather than dry, logical exposition, theology in Buechner's mode tugs at the heartstrings of our life, and pulls us toward discovering what it is like to believe. Faith in God looms as that horizon hovering on the edges of our awareness that shapes all our seeing and doing. And what we glimpse ordinarily and only occasionally out of the corner of an eye leaps to stage center. We find ourselves no longer looking *at* the reality to which Buechner points but looking *through* his stories so that we dwell in them and in the reality they depict. To paraphrase Robert Browning we could say of what Buechner does, "Ah, but the reach should exceed the grasp, or what's a meta-phor?" And in this biblical way, it may be more accurate to speak of Buechner as a theologian than to use the term to describe many a contemporary rationalist who belongs to the guilds of academic theology.

Roger Jones, from the perspective of the physical sciences, writes, "I define metaphor as an evocation of the inner connection among things. It is an art of consciousness that borders on the very creation of things, blurring the distinctions between them, even between them and their names."[12] This way of understanding metaphor is close to Buechner's and illumines how creative art underlies all naming and evoking.

In Buechner's hands, for example, *The Wizard of Oz* becomes a metaphor for the whole of human life, and he works out what he understands this can mean in his novel *The Entrance to Porlock*.

To say that theology takes the form of metaphor for Buechner underscores his awareness of the central place artistic work has in shaping the vision of reality toward which we live. Buechner is constantly about the task of prodding us to *see.* Artistry takes on theological depth and meaning, and theology is clothed with artistic delicacy and power in Buechner's hands.

"Glory is to God what style is to an artist," Buechner writes, and continues:

A painting by Vermeer, a sonnet by Donne, a Mozart aria — each is so rich with the style of the one who made it that to the connoisseur it couldn't have been made by anybody else, and the effect is staggering. The style of an artist brings you as close to the sound of his voice and the light in his eyes as it is possible to get this side of actually shaking hands with him.

In the words of the nineteenth Psalm, "The heavens are telling the glory of God." It is the same thing. To the connoisseur not just sunsets and starry nights but dust storms, rain forests, garter snakes, the human face, are all unmistakably the work of a single hand. . . . To behold God's glory, to sense God's style, is the closest you can get to God this side of Paradise, just as to read *King Lear* is the closest you can get to Shakespeare.

Glory is what God looks like when for the time being all you have to look at God with is a pair of eyes. (*WT*, 30)

Language about God or to describe the divine presence in human life and experience is, for Buechner, always metaphorical. Words themselves are metaphors for the reality that we feel immersed in and that we live toward because we believe in it. We can only say, in metaphorical form, what we believe God is like.

The reason for this is simply that the term *God* refers to that reality in whom we believe we live and move and have our being. God signifies a level of meaning that encompasses, grounds, and is the originating source of all human meanings. "It is as impossible," writes Buechner, ". . . to demonstrate the existence of God as it would be for even Sherlock Holmes to demonstrate the existence of Arthur Conan Doyle" (*WT*, 31).

Theology as it appears in the biblical materials is embodied in vivid and variegated metaphors. Thus the Bible, as Buechner points out, is filled with stories, parables, and historical narrative describing in metaphorical ways who God is and what God's action is in creation, history, and human interaction. God is depicted as present in the life of Israel, in Jesus Christ, and in human lives lived in community.

Here is an example of one biblical story and what Buechner does with it. It appears in the meditation that provides the title for *The*

Magnificent Defeat. The story is about Jacob's wrestling with the angel, "an ancient, jagged-edged story, dangerous and crude as a stone knife," (*MD,* 11) Buechner says in introducing it. After deceiving his old father, Isaac, and getting the inheritance rightly due his brother, Esau, Jacob wisely leaves the vicinity, goes to the hill country, marries, becomes rich, and then returns to claim the land that God promised to Abraham, Isaac, and now Jacob as a gift. "When he reaches the river Jabbok, which is all that stands between him and the promised land," Buechner says in taking up the narrative, "he sends his family and his servants across ahead of him, but he remains to spend the night on the near shore alone." Buechner speculates why: "Maybe in order to savor to its fullest this moment of greatest achievement, this moment for which all his earlier moments have been preparing and from which only a river separates him now."

> And then it happens. Out of the deep of the night a stranger leaps. He hurls himself at Jacob, and they fall to the ground, their bodies lashing through the darkness. It is terrible enough not to see the attacker's face, and his strength is more terrible still, the strength of more than a man. All the night through they struggle in silence until just before morning when it looks as though a miracle might happen. Jacob is winning. The stranger cries out to be set free before the sun rises. Then, suddenly, all is reversed.
> He merely touches the hollow of Jacob's thigh, and in a moment Jacob is lying there crippled and helpless. The sense we have, which Jacob must have had, [is] that the whole battle was from the beginning fated to end this way, that the stranger had simply held back until now, letting Jacob exert all his strength and almost win so that when he was defeated, he would know that he was truly defeated. (*MD,* 17–18)

Beaten and exhausted, Jacob hangs on and cries, "I will not let you go, unless you bless me!" It will not be a blessing, Buechner notes, "that he can have now by the strength of his cunning or the force of his will, but a blessing that he can have only as a gift."

> Power, success, happiness, as the world knows them, are his who will fight for them hard enough; but peace, love, joy, are only from God. And God is the enemy whom Jacob fought there by the

river, of course, and whom in one way or another we all of us fight—God, the beloved enemy. Our enemy because, before giving us everything, [God] demands of us everything.

After highlighting and enriching the metaphors already present in the story as told in Genesis, Buechner adds this cascade of images to conclude the meditation:

Only remember the last glimpse that we have of Jacob, limping home against the great conflagration of the dawn. Remember Jesus of Nazareth, staggering on broken feet out of the tomb toward the Resurrection, bearing on his body the proud insignia of the defeat which is victory, the magnificent defeat of the human soul at the hands of God. (*MD,* 18)

Even all the means used in Scripture, powerful as they are, do not suffice to express the overwhelming experience of God. The discursive forms theology has usually taken in the Western tradition of Christianity, however, are far weaker and paler than the metaphorical ways of story, song, and history that the Bible uses to speak of God. "All-wise. All-powerful. All-loving. We bore both God and ourselves with our chatter. God cannot be expressed but only experienced," Buechner reminds us. As we reach into the depth of what we experience and tell the meaning we find there with enough artistic power to reach into the experience of others, theology rooted in real believing becomes possible and just may happen now and then in the midst of our sacred journeys.

Buechner adds: "In the last analysis, you cannot pontificate but only point. A Christian is one who points at Christ and says, 'I can't prove a thing, but there's something about his eyes and his voice. There's something about the way he carries his head, his hands, the way he carries his cross—the way he carries me.'" (*WT,* 32)

Buechner is by no means alone in understanding theology as metaphorical. A recent movement in Christian theology is turning away from exclusive reliance on philosophical method and rational discourse to narrative and parable as the most profound and enduring form of theology.

This view is held by philosophers as well as theologians. For example, Michael Polanyi sees clearly the capacity of art to convey theological depth in ways that are impossible for rational discursiveness. He writes:

> Music, poetry, painting: the arts—whether abstract or representative—are a dwelling in and a breaking out which lie somewhere between science and worship. . . . Owing to its sensuous content a work of art can affect us far more comprehensively than a mathematical theorem. Moreover, artistic creation and enjoyment are contemplative experience more akin than mathematics to religious communion. Art, like mysticism, breaks through the screen of objectivity and draws on our pre-conceptual capacities of contemplative vision. Poetry "purges from our inward sight the film of familiarity which obscures from us the wonder of our being," it breaks into "a world to which the familiar world is chaos." (Shelley)[13]

In this perspective the whole creation is active, filled with tensions and suspense, with surprise and disappointment, with the comic and tragic, groaning in travail and being made new from the womb of what already is. We are part of that process, and through the dramatic metaphors of artists we can come alive to our possibilities for living deeply and abundantly. Artistic and metaphorical theology can help us, in Amos Wilder's words, to build up an unseen "coral reef" of sensibility in the soul, "an edifice wrought indeed out of the common realities, but set in new relations, bathed in the light of the imagination, transfigured not into a false unreality but into their true significance."[14]

The distinctiveness of Buechner is that he not only knows the theological power of metaphors in stories told with artistic force and set within a comprehensive religious vision; he is also capable of exemplifying this insight with sensitivity and brilliance in his writings.

For example, there is this passage from the musings of the hundred-year-old sinner/saint Godric:

> I've lived at Finchale fifty years, and thus my near a hundred, give or take, are split in two. The first half teems with places that I saw and deeds I did and folk I knew. The second half I've dwelled here by myself. Three times only have I left, such as the day I went to Christmas Mass at Durham. Except for those the monks give plaited crosses to, I've scarcely seen a living soul apart from

Reginald, and Ailred now and then, and Perkin, God be praised. The lad is twenty-some and started bringing eggs to me when he himself was little bigger than an egg. So, by the reckoning of men, one half my life has been an empty box. Yet if they only understood, it's been the fuller of the two. Three things I've filled it with: *what used to be, what might have been,* and, for the third, *what may be yet* and in some measure *is* already had we only eyes to see. (*G,* 139)

The metaphor of the empty box is simple, though apt and illuminating. At times, from Buechner's first novel onward, the metaphors and similes are numerous and often subtle, interlocking, and complex. Later we shall look more carefully at the wholeness of this creative artistry in the use of metaphor.

As we seek to express the reality in which we believe most deeply today, it is not only thoroughly appropriate, in Buechner's view, to use metaphors; we *must* use them as well as other artistic images of various kinds. Fresh perspectives are needed in order to infuse old words and concepts with new life and meaning. Buechner's metaphors cut through the worn-out trappings of abstract religious language and set us off on paths of association that widen our awareness of what faith means and how best we can express it.

With his insight into the metaphorical character of all human expressions of faith in God, through his perspective on art as incarnating our comprehensive views of life and reality in the images it uses, and by means of his ability to create stories that function as parables of life's larger meaning, Buechner binds art and theology together in a covenant that resonates with biblical faith even as it displays the power of a consummate artist. With this overall understanding, I shall turn now to the elements that go into the makeup of Buechner as novelist/theologian.

CHAPTER 2

The Impulse to Write

In a perceptive article on Buechner, James Woelfel says, "Buechner is not only a good novelist . . . he is also a rare combination of literary artist and creative theologian, which should make him of special interest to the theological community."[15] By now it ought to be clear that, for the most part, I agree with Woelfel. Buechner's writing brings together gifts and insights that I find all too seldom, a compound that seems to me desperately needed in our world. He is an artist/novelist with amazing gifts of imagination, style, and human insight; a preacher/theologian who not only understands the Gospel and Christian faith, but can make it live for us through evocative story and symbol. And he is a person able to reflect on what he does in his artistic work and to articulate his own experience in such a way that we believe maybe we can do the same in relation to our own lives.

I want to be sure, however, that we do not view Buechner's art as only a better way to express theological convictions. Woelfel's perspective suggests why theologians would do well to pay attention to Buechner. It also enables us to see how he fits in with the growing movement in theology to turn toward narrative as a replacement for, or supplement to, the rational modes of discourse usual in academic Western theology. But that point of view can easily lead us to undervalue him as an artist. Buechner is a novelist/theologian, not a theologian who uses novels to improve the way he articulates doctrine.

I want to be equally sure that artists, writers of fiction in particular, understand that Buechner's work shows the deeper dimensions of artistic action, how art inevitably expresses convictions, and the creative ways in which those convictions can emerge. To put it a different way, he illumines the theological horizons of art and human living. Buechner's work cannot be reduced to religious themes in narrative disguise, nor is Buechner an artist who uses ultimate concerns to enliven his stories and appeal to a wider audience. As a novelist/theologian, his art and theology are coordinate; his faith and fiction become integrally united through his artistic powers and profound personal commitment.

Although the details of Buechner's life story may help us to understand something of the process by which he has come to represent in his own being that fusion of art and religion that leads me to call him a novelist/theologian, we have not yet explored what goes into his writing and how he goes about it. In this chapter we shall look at what he says about influences on him, how he got started writing, why he writes, where his ideas come from—and try to listen through and beyond the words he uses for the core of meaning that draws out the artist within him and evokes the impulse to write.

Though Buechner's roots as a writer are clearly in his own life and experience, he adds to this context rich resources from the Western cultural heritage and from special sectors of the literary tradition to which he was attracted in college, seminary, and in the years since. I shall list many, many influences, indicating the names of people and books he mentions here and there. Not all of these sources can be explored in detail. But in them we can perhaps discern the elusive seedbeds of his storytelling: his love of language, his vivid imagination, and the unpredictable world of his ineradicable, inarticulate dreaming.

MENTORS, LITERARY INFLUENCES,
AND OTHER SOURCES OF INSPIRATION

"I have always loved fairy tales," Buechner says, "and to this day read E. Nesbit and the Oz books, Andrew Lang and the Narnia books and Tolkien with more intensity that I read almost anything else" (*AG,* 41). When we examine the sources of his ideas, fairy tales and their authors must be high on the list. But that is only a beginning. The list can be lengthened greatly simply by adding the influences that Buechner names in his autobiographic works. The names that follow, I feel, offer a fascinating collection and a helpful point of beginning for understanding the varied, even strange, places in which Buechner finds inspiration.

Sources he mentions include this varied lot: Charles Dickens, Robert Graves, G. K. Chesterton, Graham Greene, paintings (especially from *A Treasury of Art Masterpieces*), Wagner's operas, William Shakespeare, Dante, St. Francis, William Blake, T. S. Eliot, Jane

Austen, C. S. Lewis, Dostoevsky, Arthur Koestler, Arthur Miller, James Joyce, Pär Lagerkvist, Albert Camus, Jean-Paul Sartre, Joan of Arc, Buddhism, Gertrude Stein, George Buttrick, Reinhold Niebuhr, Paul Tillich, James Muilenburg, Agnes Sanford, Karl Barth, Friedrich Schleiermacher, Annie Dillard, Ralph Abernathy, Samuel Taylor Coleridge, Henry Ward Beecher, Leo Tolstoy, Mark Twain, Michelangelo, Louis Armstrong, John Milton, Stephen Crane, Herman Melville, W. H. Auden, Robert Frost, and, especially, John Donne, Gerard Manley Hopkins, Anthony Trollope, and the Bible.

It is indeed a great cloud of witnesses. Some are accepted literary figures, the distinguished artists of past and present whom one might expect to be models for an aspiring, well-educated writer in our society. Other influences extend beyond this cultural circle but seem reasonable, given the scope of Buechner's interests. There is a sizable group remaining that might strike us as peculiar: radio shows such as "The Lone Ranger" and "Mr. Keen, Tracer of Lost Persons"; the Oz books, popular songs; movies; Buechner's family; hymns; and, of course, Mrs. Taylor, of whom I shall have more to say later.

Consider, for example, the Oz books. One has only to read *The Entrance to Porlock* in order to realize the significant impact upon him of that realm of fantasy created by L. Frank Baum. "Reading an Oz book," Buechner tells us, "was like seeing a movie where the illusion of reality is so complete that, even beyond the doors of the set that are not opened, and around the bends of roads where your eye cannot see, you have utter faith that the world of the drama goes on with as much reality as the world itself" (*SJ*, 15).

More than that, however, the Oz stories, in a way similar to, and parallel with, the Bible, permeate Buechner's artistic vision. He is constantly discovering and revealing to us the realms of mystery and magic to be found hidden within the prosaic Kansas of everyday experience. Our own world becomes like that land a place where the real magic is so mixed with the fraudulent as often to become indistinguishable. Oz and the Emerald City appear early, in *The Seasons' Difference*, that book haunted by mystic vision, and continue to shape Buechner's work.

And then there are the radio programs. Rather than growing up and putting away childish things, Buechner has brought childhood fantasies with him. As a result his world is like a snowman, made of rolled-up accumulations of experiences stacked on one another and topped with human features and a ridiculous hat. The Lone Ranger, masked and mysterious, with the loyal Tonto at his side, rides in and out of Buechner's fiction, though his exploits there are never so unambiguously successful as in his radio incarnation. Mr. Keen, Tracer of Lost Persons, wanders around in Buechner's stories in more disguises than Sherlock Holmes thought to use. Indeed, Buechner as author is forever a Lone Ranger trying to right the injustices and ills of a fallen world, and therefore is always also seeking to be that agent by whom lost persons may discover themselves to be found. In ways poignantly similar to those of Holden Caulfield, Buechner wants to be a "catcher in the rye."

His teachers at Union made their mark on the religious seeker and thirsty theological novice who came from George Buttrick's church to study. James Muilenburg's prophetic style, personal passion, and fusion of faith with biblical fantasy influenced Buechner almost beyond telling. If we cease looking for outward resemblance, then in addition to Dr. Kuykendall in *The Return of Ansel Gibbs*, Theodore Nicolet, Peter Ringkoping, Leo Bebb, and Godric all have something of Muilenburg's spirit within them. And Paul Tillich's theological insights pervade Buechner's thinking, nowhere more clearly than in the interrelationship of religion, art, and creativity.

Among literary influences, Donne, Hopkins, and Trollope are probably the most important. I shall say something about each of them at appropriate points further along.

There are other writers who are capable of miracles like Buechner's in combining faith and art. I think of Dostoevsky, Charles Williams, C. S. Lewis, Georges Bernanos, Friedrich Dürrenmatt, Annie Dillard, Alan Paton, and Thornton Wilder. Buechner himself notes his own similarity to Graham Greene. Of the alcoholic Roman Catholic priest in *The Power and the Glory*, he says that Greene demonstrates that "the power and the glory of God are so overwhelming that they can shine forth into the world through even such a one as this seedy, alcoholic little failure of a man who thus, less by any virtue of his own than by the sheer power of grace within him, becomes a kind of saint at the end" (*SJ*, 17–18). Buechner has also been quoted as saying, "I sometimes think my whole literary life has been an effort to rewrite *The Power and the Glory* in a way of my own. Part of what I was about in the Bebb books was to create a kind of whiskey priest."[16]

In many ways, however, Buechner reminds me especially of Søren

Kierkegaard, the great Danish thinker, who combined religious faith and artistic expression. Both carry out their ministries primarily through writing, and both are superb artist/theologians. Much of Kierkegaard's work was aesthetic in form, stories for the most part. In these writings, Christian faith was affirmed through character, action, and metaphor. Like Buechner, Kierkegaard also published sermons and meditations. The central issue of Kierkegaard's authorship was attempting to give fresh, meaningful statement to the stale, formal religiosity of the established Christianity of nineteenth-century Denmark. As Kierkegaard put the issue, "How does one become a Christian in Christendom?" Buechner asks the same questions and offers some provocative possibilities for us today.

There are also many differences, beyond their being in different cultures and different centuries. Kierkegaard was brought up within the church and, in accordance with the wishes of his father, trained in theology. Buechner, on the other hand, was reared in a family that had little to do with the church; only after the crisis of his conversion experience did he attend seminary. Two major crises influenced Kierkegaard's life decisively. One occurred long before he was born, when his father as a boy, crushed beneath the load of poverty and hard work on the harsh moors of Jutland, cursed God and carried an even more crushing weight of guilt for the rest of his life. He passed it on to his son Søren. The second crisis occurred when Kierkegaard, after deciding not to become ordained, broke off his engagement with Regine Olsen, whom he continued to love for the remainder of his life. By contrast, Buechner's own crisis led him to become ordained. And he has long been happily married.

Kierkegaard and Buechner make an interesting pair. I shall compare and contrast them further in the next chapter.

From these examples of the varied influences on Buechner, you get an idea of the far out, and nearby, sources on which he draws and the fascinating changes wrought in them by Buechner's religiously childlike imagination.

LOVE OF LANGUAGE AND STORYTELLING

This seems to be where it all begins for Buechner—with a spell that words cast over him so that they enter his imagination and take on a transformed life of their own in him. Under their power he becomes enchanted with naming and putting words together in ways that bring new wonders into being. In his autobiographical accounts he recalls people and times that, in marvelous ways, fed his love of language.

There is, for example, Mrs. Taylor, referred to earlier as an influence on him. She was a nurse who looked after him and his brother when they were children and Buechner's father was working in Washington, D.C. Mrs. Taylor was capable of entertaining children, an ability probably cultivated both as a professional skill and as defensive device. Quite clearly, her talents were not wasted on young Freddy Buechner.

In the brick-walled garden of the Buechner home in Georgetown one day, Mrs. Taylor said to him, "'Now I am going to show you something that you have never seen before.' Then she opened her mouth wide and sang out a single loud, clear note, and as she held it, her teeth dropped a full half an inch before my marveling eyes. She was right. I had never seen such a thing before" (*SJ*, 13).

Mrs. Taylor opened up the developing imagination of the precocious preschooler and, in Buechner's remembering, contributed to his store of vivid ideas and early start on his way with words. Buechner relates that another time Mrs. Taylor

> showed me a cut of raw beefsteak and, pointing to a small knot of white gristle somewhere toward the center, said, "That is the soul. Now you know what a soul looks like." She had a suitcase too, with a knife in it which she said had killed a Mexican, and she had something made out of glass that she said I was not old enough yet to see. She cut the pictures of things and the names of things out of magazines for me to paste in a scrapbook and taught me that way how to read and write when I was five. (*SJ*, 13)

In her own special way Mrs. Taylor helped lay the foundation for Buechner's preoccupation with religious themes in general and with Christian faith in particular. Buechner tells how after his brother and he were in bed in the evening, Mrs. Taylor would lie down next to them in the dusk and sing songs with them. Two songs they sang most often were "The Spanish Cavalier" and "The Old Rugged Cross," which, Buechner says, "as far as I can remember was the only hymn I ever heard as the child of non-church-going parents, although I had no idea what a hymn was or what a cross was or why it was something to sing about in the dark" (*SJ*, 13).

From her he began to learn the art of naming and the power of language to relate us to things and also to control them. Buechner writes:

> She was my mentor, my miracle-worker, and the mother of much that I was and in countless unrecognizable ways probably still am, yet I don't know where she came from or anything about her life apart from the few years of it that she spent with us. Nor do I know what became of her after she left, and there is a sadness in not knowing, in thinking of all the mothers and fathers we have all of us had who, for the little we remember them, might as well never have existed at all except for the deep and hidden ways in which they exist in us still. In any case, Mrs. Taylor was the one who vastly increased my dominion over the earth and its creatures by teaching me the art of naming them. It was not till years later that I learned what a fatal art that is because if, on the one hand, to name a thing is to be able to address it, to appropriate it, to have a way of understanding it, it is, on the other hand, to erect a barrier between yourself and it which only on the rarest and most inspired occasions are you ever able to surmount again. Now that, thanks to Mrs. Taylor, I can name a tree as a tree, what I see when I look at it is less what it actually is than simply the name I name it by. When I was a child, what I saw when I looked at a tree was something as naked in its mystery as I was naked in mine. Yet I thank her anyway. If she had not taught me the names, somebody else would have, and probably not half so well. (*SJ*, 13–14)

He writes also about the class in which he was a student at Lawrenceville School that was "a course less in literature than in language and the great power that language has to move and in some measure even to transform the human heart" (*SJ*, 69). His teacher, Mr. Martin, had, Buechner recalls, "a tremendous, Irishman's zest for the blarney and wizardry of words." He continues:

> I had always been a reader and loved words for the tales they can tell and the knowledge they can impart and the worlds they can conjure up like the Scarecrow's Oz and Claudius's Rome; but this teacher, Mr. Martin, was the first to give me a feeling for what words are, and can do, in themselves. Through him I started to sense that words not only convey something, but *are* something; that words have

color, depth, texture of their own, and the power to evoke vastly more than they mean; that words can be used not merely to make things clear, make things vivid, make things interesting and whatever else, but to make things happen inside the one who reads them or hears them. (*SJ*, 68)

What happened to Buechner at Lawrenceville School is an earlier parallel to the later experience of conversion, and it may be of almost equal importance. If that time when Jesus was crowned in his heart among confession and tears and great laughter gave Buechner a Gospel to proclaim, it was in his time with Mr. Martin that he discovered the medium in which he was called to work in carrying out the proclamation. "We search, on our journeys," Buechner writes, "for a self to be, for other selves to love, and for work to do" (*SJ*, 72). He continues several pages later:

> By the time I was sixteen, I knew as surely as I knew anything that the work I wanted to spend my life doing was the work of words. I did not yet know what I wanted to say with them. I did not yet know in what form I wanted to say it or to what purpose. But if a vocation is as much the work that chooses you as the work you choose, then I knew from that time on that my vocation was, for better or worse, to involve that searching for, and treasuring, and telling of secrets which is what the real business of words is all about. (*SJ*, 74–75)

Artists are ever on a treasure hunt, attempting to uncover within themselves the secrets of the human heart and to tell them in powerful ways that lead others to make similar discoveries in their own experience. The inner meaning of those secrets would grasp Buechner later in a pew in a church on Madison Avenue, and its outward form would emerge in his novels and in his nonfiction with an artistry that would draw us into the context of his own vision, inviting us to share it.

In a passage from a recent essay, Buechner provides an interesting insight into what he understands is going on as a writer uses words:

> Writers travel through life like the rest of us, seeing the sights and responding to them in all sorts of inner ways, and then, like the rest of us, they need, in their loneliness, to put it into words. Like God saying "Let there be light" so that by naming it he can bring it into

being, the writers of literature say "Let it be *this*"— this putting into words of their experience of life — so that it can more fully and effectively *be* both for themselves and for the rest of us. (*RCR*, 179)

A SPECIAL WAY WITH WORDS

People often speak of a particular passage as being "vintage Buechner." By this they mean that it represents his very distinctive way of using language. Often it is writing that is funny. In *Wishful Thinking*, for example, he tells us, "Contrary to Mrs. Grundy, sex is not sin. Contrary to Hugh Hefner, it's not salvation either. Like nitroglycerin, it can used either to blow up bridges or heal hearts" (*WT*, 87). He can also be provocative: "The preacher pulls the little cord that turns on the lectern light and deals out his note cards like a riverboat gambler. The stakes have never been higher" (*TT*, 23). And sometimes the way of putting things that is so characteristic of Buechner can be breath-catching, as in this example from *The Final Beast*.

"Nicolet, I may adopt you," says Lillian Flagg, the religious counselor that Nicolet's unhappy parishioner Rooney Vail has come to Muscadine to see. Troubled by an act of adultery in her past, Rooney has fled from husband and home in the little New England town of Myron, seeking help. Her pastor, Theodore Nicolet, has gone in search of her and has found her at the home of Lillian Flagg, who is talking to Nicolet while Rooney is upstairs.

She ran her hands briskly up and down her bare arms, never taking her eyes from him. "Oh Lord, how advice bores me, especially when it's good. And yours was good enough. 'Go back to your husband.' That probably didn't come so easy, did it? 'Forget your infidelity.' She told me, you see. It's so modern, and it's so sane, and it's just the advice she'd want if she wanted advice. Only give her what she really wants, Nicolet."

"Give her what, for Christ's sake?"

"For Christ's sake . . ." Lillian Flagg took a deep breath, then let it out slowly, shaking her head. "The only thing you have to give." And then she almost shouted at him. "Forgive her for Christ's sake, little priest!"

"But she knows I forgive her."

"She doesn't know God forgives her. That's the only power you

have—to tell her that. Not just that he forgives her the poor little
adultery. But the faces she can't bear to look at now. The man's.
Her husband's. Her own, half the time. Tell her God forgives her
for being lonely and bored, for not being full of joy with a houseful
of children. That's what sin really is. You know—not being full of
joy. Tell her that sin is forgiven because whether she knows it or not,
that's what she wants more than anything else—what all of us want.
What on earth do you think you were ordained for?" (*FB*, 114–5)

For most of his life, Buechner has been aware of the importance of
words and his own abilities with them. In *The Sacred Journey* he
recalls:

> "You have a way with words," my instructor, the critic R. P.
> Blackmur, told me, and although at the time it was like getting the
> Pulitzer Prize, it seems to me now that there was also a barb to his
> remark. I wrote poems with punch lines, had a way of making
> words ring out and dance a little, but there was little if any of my
> life's blood in my poems. I was writing for my teachers, for glory.
> (*SJ*, 80–81)

Even earlier, however, he reports that as a child he had some sense
that there was something different about him. "I knew, as I had not
before, the sound of my own voice both literally and figuratively—
knew something of what was different about my way of speaking from
anybody else's way" (*SJ*, 72–73).

Quite clearly, he became aware early on in his life that he had a way
with words. But then, along the way, suddenly, yet over time and
through experiences that shook him and reshaped his perspective,
Buechner found an angle of vision for seeing life that filled his "way
with words" with his own life's blood.

Many writers contributed to Buechner's style as he developed his
special word-ways; three—Gerard Manley Hopkins, John Donne, and
Anthony Trollope, as I suggested earlier—deserve particular attention.
Of Hopkins, Buechner writes:

> When Gerard Manley Hopkins writes a poem about a black-
> smith and addresses him as one who "didst fettle for the great gray
> drayhorse his bright and battering sandal," he is not merely bringing

the blacksmith to life, but in a way is bringing us to life as well. Through the sound, rhythm, passion of his words, he is bringing to life in us, as might otherwise never have been brought to life at all, a sense of the uniqueness and mystery and holiness not just of the blacksmith and his great gray drayhorse, but of reality itself, including the reality of ourselves. (*SJ*, 68–69)

We sense of what Buechner learned from Hopkins and also that which he added to create something distinctively his own. Even in speaking of Hopkins, some vintage Buechner emerges.

Donne, we should remember, is, like Buechner, a preacher with great artistic powers. Buechner has much to say about him and his power with words. In an essay entitled "The Speaking and Writing of Words," Buechner writes, "We are not content merely to name what is going on inside ourselves but seek to use words that to a degree enable others to feel what it is like to live inside our skins. . . ."

> When it comes to spoken words, there are all sorts of auxiliary ways of doing this, of course — the tone of voice, facial expression, gesture and all the non-verbal sounds we make to convey something much richer and more compelling than mere intellectual meaning. And when it comes to conveying this same richness through the written word, there are needless to say a great many other devices to replace the nonverbal ones, as no one knew better, for instance, than such a great prose stylist as John Donne. (*RCR*, 174)

And then Buechner proceeds to quote a passage from one of Donne's sermons and provide a detailed analysis of how Donne uses metaphors, rhythm, iambic beat, a catch of breath, alliteration, and the special shape, color, weight, and texture of words. It is an amazing lesson in how feelings can be transmitted from one person to others through the written and spoken word (see *RCR*, 174–7).

Buechner's deeper tribute to Donne may occur in the passage where he recounts the first time, in *Lion Country*, that Antonio Parr and Sharon, Leo Bebb's daughter, make love together in the Salamander Motel in Armadillo, Florida. When he tries to tell what happened, he resorts to the words of Donne:

If I tried, I suppose I could remember how it all went, one thing leading to another thing, and when it comes my time to die and my whole life passes before me as they say a life does, I suppose I will see it all again and remember how it was with us there and what we did and what we said, which was not much, and how all the time the electric fan was going and if we had stopped to notice, we would have seen whatever there is to see of a sunset when the Venetian blinds are down. But "O my America! My new-found land," Donne wrote to his mistress on going to bed, that strange man, part priest and part satyr, who all his life was half in love with death. "My Myne of precious stones, My Emperie." And then "How blest am I in this discovering thee! To enter in these bonds is to be free. Full nakedness! All joyes are due to thee." Anything I might add to that would have to be on the order of footnotes. (*LC* in *BB*, 75–76)

Thornton Wilder says, "literature has always more resembled a torchrace than a furious dispute among heirs," so Buechner builds on Donne and Donne is lifted to new heights of meaning today. And we are brought to dwell more fully in the embodied, incarnate character of our humanity.

What Buechner has to say about Trollope indicates the great impact the English writer has had and continues to have on him. At no point is that influence stronger than in Buechner's identification with the vocation Trollope has in view for himself. In a passage from Trollope's autobiography that Buechner quotes, Trollope says that many "look upon the tellers of stories as among the tribe of those who pander to the wicked pleasures of a wicked world. I have ever thought of myself as a preacher of sermons, and my pulpit as one which I could make both salutary and agreeable to my audience" (quoted *RCR*, 178). This is the vocation Buechner has made his own, the combination of the callings of writer and minister.

"Words—especially religious words, words, that have to do with the depth of things—get tired and stale the way people do," Buechner says. "Find new words or put old words together in combinations that make them heard as new, make yourself new, and make you understand in new ways" (*NT*, 93). That is the reason Buechner cultivates carefully his way with words and that is why, I am convinced, his vision and his abilities are needed so much today.

A LUMP IN THE THROAT

In one of the most vivid ways he uses to tell us the source of the impulse for his writing, Buechner speaks of an experience we have all had, though not usually with such creative results. "Since my ordination, as well as before," he writes, "novels, for me, start—as Robert Frost said his poems did—with a lump in the throat." (*NT*, 59). It is from this feeling that his characters emerge and the plots of his fiction take shape. This impulse goes hand in hand with his emphasis on listening to our lives. "I try to be as true as I can to life as I have known it. I write not as a propagandist but as an artist" (*NT*, 59).

The lump in the throat of the artist—the something that has so moved him or her—is the source for Buechner. He then transfers the lump into the throats of his characters, and from there it becomes a lump in the throats of his readers. An illustration appears in *The Alphabet of Grace* as Buechner discusses the origins of a scene in *The Final Beast*.

> In the case of this scene, I, as the novelist, was being quite direct. In just such a place on just such a day I lay down in the grass with just such wild expectations. Part of what it means to believe in God, at least part of what it means for me, is to believe in the possibility of miracle, and because of a variety of circumstances I had a very strong feeling at that moment that the time was ripe for miracle, my life was ripe for miracle, and the very strength of the feeling itself seemed a kind of vanguard of miracle. (*AG*, 7)

The lump is there in a very real situation in Buechner's life. And from the lump in his throat arises a sense of yearning and expectancy, yearning for meaning and the hope that the miracle of meaning could actually happen. In this situation when Buechner was waiting and hoping for some sign from God, something occurred, but it was quite different from anything he had expected. Instead of a brilliant light from heaven or a sonorous voice addressing him, he heard two branches of an apple tree knocking together, making a dry, distinct sound.

Out of this remembered experience, when a lump in the throat arose from his faith and his hope, his artistic imagination created the passage in which Theodore Nicolet, the young minister in *The Final Beast*, away from home, is lying in the grass behind the barn at his father's house. As Buechner puts it, there "certain things happen and do not happen."

> He closed his eyes in the warm sunlight . . . and the earth beneath him seemed to tilt this way and that like a great disc. There was the smell of oranges, his arms heavy as stone on the grass. He could hear the buzz of the yellow jackets drifting over the compost. Death must come like this. The Reverend Nicolet found behind his father's boardinghouse, no sign of struggle. . . . Only it was not death that was coming, whatever else. His heart pounded, and he did not dare open his eyes not from fear of what he might see but of what he might not see, so sure now, crazily, that if ever it was going to happen, whatever it was that happened—*joy, Nicolet, joy*—it must happen now in this unlikely place as always in unlikely places: the road to Damascus, Emmaus, Muscadine, stuffy roomful of frightened Jews smelling of fish. (*FB*, 175–6)

The same believing and hoping and expectancy are present as were present for Buechner. What happens, or does not happen, also takes place within the context of ordinary human experience, but experience made luminous by imaginative faith and by a yearning that caused a real pain in Buechner's throat. Buechner continues the account of Nicolet's experience:

> "Please," he whispered. Still flat on his back, he stretched out his fists as far as they would reach—"Please . . ."—then opened them, palms up, and held them there as he watched for something, for the air to cleave, fold back like a tent flap, to let a splendor through. You prayed to the Christ in the people you knew, the living and the dead: what should you do, who should you be? And sometimes they told you. But to pray now this other prayer, not knowing what you were asking, only "Please, please . . ." Somewhere a screen door slammed, and all the leaves were still except for one that fluttered like a bird's wing.
>
> "Please come," he said, then "Jesus," swallowing, half blind with the sun in his eyes as he raised his head to look. The air would part like a curtain, and the splendor would not break or bend anything but only fill the empty places between the trees, the trees and the house, between his hands which he brought together now. . . .

Two apple branches struck against each other with the limber clack of wood on wood. That was all—a tick-tock rattle of branches—but then a fierce lurch of excitement at what was only daybreak, only the smell of summer coming, only starting back again for home, but oh Jesus, he thought, with a great lump in his throat and a crazy grin, it was an agony of gladness and beauty falling wild and soft like rain. Just clack-clack, but praise God, he thought. Praise God. Maybe all his journeying, he thought, had been only to bring him here to hear two branches hit each other twice like that, to see nothing cross the threshold but to see the threshold, to hear the dry clack-clack of the world's tongue at the approach of the approach perhaps of splendor. (*FB*, 176–8)

Those apple branches hitting together with such amazing results came first from Buechner's experience of a lump in the throat. Then it became a great lump and a crazy grin for Nicolet. When I encountered that passage as I was reading *The Final Beast*, it gave me a lump in the throat and goose bumps all over. And it does the same for others when I read Buechner's experience as it has entered Nicolet's in the novel. The words evoke the same deep feelings for others that Buechner first felt, transposed with his artistic magic into an event in the life of a troubled young pastor, and makes the same experience occur for me and many more as they read or hear.

It took, of course, much more than two branches hitting together for it to become an experience of God for Buechner. There also had to be the readiness, the faithful waiting and hoping, and the imagination to be able to hear with joy and then respond. The lump in the throat must not be viewed in isolation from the context of Buechner's life and artistic power. As they emerge in his writing, those lumps in his throat prove for Buechner to be rich seedbeds of art and theology in close harmony.

THE PLACE WHERE DREAMS COME FROM

Concerning the character Leo Bebb, focus of four novels, Buechner writes, "He came, unexpected and unbidden, from a part of myself no less mysterious and inaccessible than the part where dreams come from" (*NT*, 97). In the introduction to *The Book of Bebb*, he says something more that throws light on the elusive sources of his impulse to write *Lion Country*:

It began in a barber shop. I picked up some dog-eared publication with snippets of hair in between the pages, and what it opened to was a news story about a man who was in trouble with the law for running some sort of religious diploma mill and had done time for something else even more baroque in the past. I don't remember any of it very clearly, but I remember some of the pictures—the man himself stuffed into a double-breasted suit, a flat-topped stucco building that he used as a church, an assistant with china teeth and a sick smile. It was all it took.

From wherever it is that dreams come from, a whole world rose up for me more or less on the spot. A seedy little jumping-off place in inland Florida and a Charles Addams manse. A smelly flight of subway stairs. Some mangy lions in an outdoor zoo. And the people rose up more or less on the spot too with faces and in some cases even names already attached. There was a bunch of eccentric Indians and a loose-limbed girl with a bootleg smile. There was an olive-skinned young drifter and introvert who looked a little like the young J. D. Salinger. There was a girl dying in a hospital with tinted windowpanes and a hypochondriac ex-husband with invisible eyebrows and eyelashes. And there was also, of course, Leo Bebb. I believe I had to think a little bit to find his name, but it came soon enough. And then his eye. I didn't have to think up having it flutter shut every once in a while. It did it all by itself while I happened to be watching. It was a wink, a kind of come-on, and it started me off on what was, literarily speaking, the great romance of my life. (*BB*, vii)

Do ideas well up like that? Do they really happen to writers as an accident happens, rather than having to be dredged up slowly and with great effort, like pulling last year's wreck out of the accumulated mud and tangle of growth at the bottom of a pond? The imagination works in that spontaneous fashion for all of us at times, so it is easy to believe that it works that way even more for others. For whatever reason of birth or training by Mrs. Taylor and the Oz books, Buechner seems to have a well-developed relation with that place deep within where dreams come from. And there staring at him one day were Leo Bebb and the entire menagerie of lions, Indians, and other tragicomic types.

Buechner says similar things about the origins of his first novel. *A Long Day's Dying*, he writes, "was in no overt way autobiographical. Instead, like all the novels I have written since, it came from the same part of myself that dreams come from and by a process scarcely less obscure. I labor very hard at the actual writing of them, but the plot and characters and general feeling of them come from somewhere deeper down and farther away than conscious effort" (*SJ*, 98).

This way of speaking is still another way Buechner describes how he writes, and it must be explored in order to understand the sources of the impulses that guide his work. Sometimes this "place where dreams come from" appears to involve daydreams. At other times, Buechner seems to mean that hidden depth from which night dreams come.

In *The Alphabet of Grace* there is a passage about the paradox of the dream world, with both its chaos and its capacity to reflect an order that transcends, rather than abolishes, our ordinary waking world. At one point he tells of dreaming that he is sitting on a stool at a bar. His glass has left a wet ring on the counter:

> With my finger, I start to move the wet around. I move it this way and that way with nothing much on my dream of a mind. And then on the smooth counter of the bar I write a name. When I have finished writing it, I start to weep, and the tears wake me up. I cannot remember the name I wrote, but I know it was a name that I would be willing to die for. Maybe it was the secret name of God or the secret name of the world. Maybe it was my own secret name. The dream is only a dream, but the tears are exceedingly real. (*AG*, 21)

This dream is used by Buechner in a somewhat altered fashion in *The Final Beast* (190) and in *Love Feast*. Antonio Parr dreams that he receives his name written on a silver dollar. But when he wakes up, he can't remember what it was (*LF* in *BB*, 342).

That illustration may be too direct to get at the sources of the materials Buechner uses in his writing. It does suggest, however, how experiences from the rich and unpredictable world of our dreaming can be transformed into a significant incident in a novel.

The transformation, however, takes imagination. And even prior to that, the dream itself, however involuntary its presence and its content may appear, involves imagination. Our dreams project worlds and possibilities that summon us to create new things. The dreaming comes from the depth of our imagination and calls forth further imagination. This ability to use the riches he finds in the place where dreams come from is one of Buechner's greatest gifts.

CHAPTER 3

The Shape of Buechner's Work

"What I set out to do," Buechner says in explaining how he wrote *The Alphabet of Grace*, "was to describe a single representative day of my life in a way to suggest what there was of God to hear in it" (*NT*, 86). This notion gave him the basic approach to the lectures. It also points to an insight that hovers around the edges of his earlier writing and influences decisively all his subsequent work. It has provided me with an important key to the shape of Buechner's entire work. As the letters of the alphabet make up words and words make up sentences and sentences are the stuff of stories, so the events of our life provide the alphabet making up our days and years and whatever meaning we find. Those same events may also spell the faith that just maybe discloses God to us.

In the introduction I told about my discovery of Frederick Buechner and the profound feelings his books evoked in me as they hurtled into my experience like stars and galaxies on a "Star Trek" voyage through space. In this chapter I want to look at his work from a different perspective. Not forgetting the way his books affect me, I now want to explore what he has written, with the purpose of discovering its shape and contours.

One way to look at the shape of Buechner's work is to view it as made up of distinct kinds of writing, what literary scholars call genres, or types. Looked at this way, Buechner's books, like Julius Caesar's Gaul, are divided into three parts: fiction, nonfiction, and autobiography. My listing of his published works that appears near the front of this book divides his work under these headings.

It has become increasingly clear to me that dealing with Buechner's work in terms of three distinct genres can lead to real misunderstanding. It is not incorrect to speak of fiction, nonfiction, and autobiography as three types of writing that Buechner produces. But it falls so far short of what he has done as to border on falsehood. His fiction has so much of himself in it that I find it best to regard it as an extension of his autobiography in deeply changed form rather than as something completely different. And his nonfictional and autobiographical writing represents so thoroughly his artistic imagination and power as to make it impossible to separate it neatly from the fiction. A different perspective is needed, I am convinced, to discern the shape of Buechner's work.

THE SHAPE OF LIFE, FAITH, GOD

If there is one thing that characterizes Buechner's writing in a distinctive way and makes him deserve the title of novelist/theologian, it is his ability to deal with the ordinary happenings of life, that alphabet of our days, and discover them spelling out the most extraordinary things in a language of grace that includes even God. In an interview in Berkeley, Buechner said, "There's a place where you hear God best in many ways. That's in your own life, which involves a conscious remembering."[17]

He shows us what this means in all his writing. Moreover, he accomplishes this with an artistic power and human sensitivity that draws us into his own life and the life of his characters until we share their experiences and begin perhaps to discern similar shapes in our own lives. Indeed, some of his experience may happen to us so vividly that our own lost or misplaced or forgotten meaning, returning from whatever far country it may have gone to, becomes found and we come a little closer to rediscovering who we are and who God is to us and for us.

Buechner's insight into seemingly mundane events and his distinctive way of reporting on these experiences illumine all things as shaped by God and disclose to us in those events the shape of God. The pattern of Buechner's alphabet, borrowing from the Hebrew—gutturals, sibilants, and the absence of vowels, as they become words, sentences, paragraphs, chapters, and books—emerges for me as a life-shape, a faith-shape, and a God-shape.

Yet that pattern is not so much the result of discovery, he insists, as it is of grace. "Grace is something you can never get but only be given," Buechner reminds us. "There's no way to earn it or deserve it or bring it about any more than you can deserve the taste of raspberries and cream or earn good looks or bring about your own birth" (*WT*, 33). Putting the bits and pieces of our lives into wholes worth living for is not something we can do for ourselves; it is a gift from God. Just as we can put the letters of the alphabet together to tell a story, so God uses the everyday, often humdrum, events of human experience to convey the meaning at the heart of the universe and God's presence in the midst of it all. For Buechner, our world is saturated with God, shaped by God, pervaded with the shape of God—if we are able to perceive it. Buechner catches up the ordinary occurrences around us and transforms them, and turns them into a looking glass that mirrors simultaneously our own true selves and the presence of God.

Earlier I said that Buechner in many ways reminded me of the Danish artist and religious thinker Søren Kierkegaard. The two ways Kierkegaard had of dealing in his writing with faith in God was through what he called indirect discourse and direct discourse. In the former mode he used artistic means to speak of faith. In order to make these writings even more indirect, he also used pseudonyms so that the public would not know that he was the author. He would even make a great show of attending musical events and then would slip out after the lights were dimmed in order to go home and work secretly on these indirect writings. But at the same time, he was publishing things in direct discourse—sermons, meditations, and so on—that expressed his Christian faith openly.

It is helpful to look at Buechner's work in terms of the distinction between indirect and direct discourse. Rather than seeing the novels as fiction, this perspective enables us to see them as indirect expression of Buechner's religious faith. The early novels appear, then, not as secular products, but rather as a way in fictional form to speak of the religious longing deep within him. After the great wall of China crumbled and Atlantis sank into the sea for him while he was listening to George Buttrick talk about the crowning of Jesus in the hearts of believers, his faith became more identifiably Christian. As he learned what this meant, through going to theological seminary and then having to articulate it in a hostile context, the faith to which he gave indirect expression in his novels took on more definite theological precision without becoming any less artistic or fictional.

In his sermons, devotional writings, and theological lectures, Buechner is engaging in what can be called direct discourse. He is expressing his Christian faith in explicit form. Yet the artistry with which he accomplishes this is no less present here than in the fiction. In both indirect and direct discourse, he is both artist and theologian.

Buechner goes beyond Kierkegaard in writing what he openly calls autobiography. Though the Danish writer approached this form in explaining the twofold nature of his work as an author, he could never have exposed himself in any form to the extent that Buechner does. Perhaps the latter's advantage is that he encountered Leo Bebb, whereas Kierkegaard never had that privilege.

As I have explored the shape of Buechner's work, however, I have discovered it necessary to view it as much more than illustrative of literary types or even indirect and direct discourse. In all that he has written, the shape of life, in some sense his own life, appears. From there the shape of human faith and Buechner's own faith come into view. And then in the midst of our own lives, bounded by the horizons of faith, the just-maybe shape of God can be glimpsed.

THE DEVELOPING PATTERN

The amount of Buechner's writing is considerable. Even more surprising is the variety he has managed to pack into the succession of books he has produced. More amazing than quantity or variety, however, are the characters he parades before us and the scenery of the worlds in which these characters dwell.

So far Buechner has published eleven novels and eleven volumes of nonfiction and autobiography. The novels range from the atmosphere of wealth, culture, and urbanity in his first ones, to the four-novel Bebb series about sleazy religiosity that maybe is something more, on to the stories of Godric, a twelfth-century saint, and Brendan, from the sixth century. Consider the characters who have taken up residence in the imagination of Buechner: Tristram Bone and Ansel Gibbs, Theodore Nicolet and Peter Ringkoping, Lucille and Brownie and Antonio and Sharon, Herman Redpath, John Turtle, the Joking Cousin, Leo Bebb himself, and Godric, to name the most prominent. It becomes clear that we are dealing not only with the place where dreams come from. We are also entering the place where wild fantasies originate, learning what kind of care and feeding nurtures them, and wondering how one mind's eye — or, better, one person's circus tent of a mind — can contain and keep in some order this procession of characters Buechner finds to inhabit his novels.

Even more amazing are the characters who roam through the works that are not fictional — Naya, Mrs. Taylor, James Muilenburg,

Grandma Buechner, George Merck, and Buechner himself, to name a few. What he exposes in these latter books rivals what is exposed in his fictional characters, including Bebb, though what he exposes is different. In the interview in Berkeley referred to earlier, Buechner says, "Self-exposure isn't the essence of what I'm doing. I'm saying some terrible things happened to me, some wonderful things happened to me. That's common to all of us. And through such events . . . something marvelous happened. And that's what I'm really talking about. It's the marvelous that I'm most interested in exposing. It's God."[18]

Many readers are inclined to think that no clear shape of God is present in Buechner's first two books. In a sense they may be correct. But there are interesting beginnings. When undeveloped film is placed in the developing tray, the images and the shape of the pictures are not visible. They appear only as the developing process unfolds. Yet the exposure of the film to light has left an implicit imprint waiting to brought to explicit view. In like manner, I believe that even the early novels have not only the shape of life about them but also the shape of faith and God.

A Long Day's Dying and *The Season's Difference* have the same brilliant style and imaginative qualities of all Buechner's work, but they lack the explicit sense of religious commitment that permeates his later writing. In these early novels the style is polished, controlled, and distant. Of *A Long's Day's Dying*, Buechner has said that "it was very dense, static, psychological, and written in such a mannered, involuted style—the residue of my romance with the seventeenth century—that it seems outrageous when I look at it now" (*SJ*, 98).

It is true that the shape of faith undergoes a great shift in subsequent novels, and God develops a more discernible shape. Though the words and style of Buechner's early novels have striking similarities with his later ones, the music of faith to which the characters dance changes dramatically. The temperature and tone shift from northeastern frigid sophistication to southern torrid downhomeyness. Nevertheless, we must not overlook a seeking for the possibility of God present from the beginning.

Even in *A Long Day's Dying*, there are hints and whispers of the shape that emerges more clearly later. Buechner speaks disparagingly of the book's style, but he also speaks of "something hiddenly at work" there:

In any case, Tristram Bone, the hero of that earliest novel, appears on the first page seated in a barber chair facing the mirror in a white sheet that hangs from his shoulders like a robe. "The mirror reflected what seemed at first a priest," is the way the book begins, and insofar as what the mirror also reflected was an image, albeit an unconscious one, of myself, I cannot help thinking of that opening sentence as itself just such a whisper, as the first faint intimation from God knows where of the direction my life was even then starting to take me, although if anyone had said so at the time, I would have thought he was mad. (*SJ*, 96)

As some hint of religious faith is a mistaken reflection in a glass dimly, so all the characters seem to struggle hopelessly with an emptiness and aloneness that isolates them from one another, yet the struggle mirrors an inner longing for an unreachable wholeness. Tristram himself tries to escape his self-preoccupation in his love for Elizabeth, but is ineffectual at communicating his feelings and only makes things worse with his well-intentioned bumbling. Elizabeth Poor, caught within a wealthy widow's sterile existence, visits her son, a student at Princeton. While there, she becomes sexually involved with a friend of her son's, a young instructor. This event provides the central turning point for the novel's action. George Motley is a successful novelist with nothing better to do than try, in his suavely demonic fashion, to make a tangled situation even worse. Only Maroo, Elizabeth's elderly mother, seems to have a larger vision that suggests the possibility of healing. Only hints and whispers, but nevertheless the shape is there, waiting for new experiences to develop it.

In Buechner's second novel, *The Seasons' Difference*, the dimension of religious faith plays a central, though ambiguous, role. If the shape of God in *A Long Day's Dying* emerges as the emptiness present in lives preoccupied with self, then God's presence in this second work of fiction is evidenced in the resistance offered to the possibility of anything as bothersome, or as threatening, as the divine.

The setting is a country house where Sam and Sara Dunn and their twelve-year-old son are vacationing. A cousin, Peter Cowley, who teaches at a boys school, is tutoring the son and six other children of nearby families. Peter has been going off with a Bible in his hand in the afternoons after his teaching is finished. One afternoon he has a vision. Disturbed, or skeptical, or both, the Dunns and some of their friends agree to go with Peter to the hillside where he had his vision to see if it will happen again. The children, annoyed at being excluded, go anyway and put on a "vision" for the adults. The novel focuses on the responses to this experience—resistance to religious complications in life, relief that there was not a real vision to contend with, and skepticism from hard-nosed William Lundrigan, a cynical book editor.

Though the vision is not repeated, Peter has not been defeated. He has compelled everyone to face the threat posed by his faith and the possibility of God's presence.

God and religious faith hang more as pall than power over these early novels. There is a curiously angled focus on meaning and spiritual transcendence that leans forward, with a sigh of near despair in the first and a cry of hope in the second, toward Buechner's conversion on Madison Avenue.

The Return of Ansel Gibbs was written mostly while in Europe for a year between his second and third years at Union Theological Seminary. In this book religion emerges with more humanity and complexity than before. Also, more of Buechner's life experience is reflected in the characters. One of the main characters resembles a professor at Union Seminary, a church in the New York slums is modeled on the East Harlem Protestant Parish where Buechner worked for a time while at Union, and the suicide of Buechner's father is dealt with in a transmuted, fictional way. Faith, life, and fiction are becoming more closely related.

Ansel Gibbs, retired from a distinguished public career, is being recalled to serve in the president's cabinet. On his way to Washington, he stops in New York to visit his daughter Anne, who is working in a church in the Harlem slums with Dr. Kuykendall, who had been an admired teacher of Ansel in college. Anne has fallen in love with Rudy Tripp, a television talk show host. Rudy's father had been a close friend of Ansel's, and Ansel has long felt indirectly responsible for the elder Tripp's suicide.

The major action of the novel comes as the result of Ansel's appearance on Rudy's television program. In the discussion on camera, seen by millions, Ansel is led into a potentially damaging discussion of his relation to the suicide of an unnamed friend (Rudy's father). Ansel wonders if Rudy has embarrassed him publicly as an act of revenge. He also concludes that he is too rational and unemotional to be fit for the cabinet post offered him. He decides to ask the president to withdraw his name. Kuykendall, Anne, and Rudy try to dissuade him. Out of this dramatic meeting, the identity crisis triggered in Ansel is resolved by a shift from distant stoicism toward a deeper awareness of his humanity and a decision to accept the cabinet position. As Ansel and Rudy are reconciled to each other through coming to terms with the suicide of Rudy's father, a powerful sense emerges that life may overcome death.

The Final Beast, the next of Buechner's novels, represents a tremendous leap forward in Buechner's distinctive combination of art and theology. His style undergoes some change. There is more bite in the sentences. Passion and commitment are present in abundance. We are brought closer to the characters because the author is closer. Buechner moves beyond any typical notions of religious language and experience, takes the raw, bleeding materials of human living in all their ambiguity, and suggests what God's presence in their midst might mean.

The shape of Theodore Nicolet's life emerges first in *The Final Beast*. Minister of a church in New England, Nicolet is a thin, youngish man "with heavy black hair and a clown's arched eyebrows and deep-set, turquoise eyes" and "a gay, foolish smile, like a drunk's or a lover's" (*FB*, 6). Nick is Bluebeard to his children, Cornelia, five, and Lizzie, three, because shaving twice a day is not enough. His wife, Franny, was killed a year previously when her car was hit by an oil truck.

One morning Irma Reinwasser, gnarled old survivor of a Nazi concentration camp and Nick's housekeeper, is disturbed to discover that Nick has gone away and that Rooney Vail, a woman in the parish, has also left town suddenly. The owner of the local newspaper, Will Poteat, for reasons of his own, has been dropping hints in his gossip column suggesting a scandalous relation between Nick and Rooney.

Rooney and Clem Vail are a couple in their mid-thirties who desperately want children and have been unable to have any. It is Rooney who attends worship most often. "There's just one reason, you know, why I come dragging in there every Sunday," she tells Nick. "I want to find out if the whole thing's true. Just *true*. That's all. Either it is or it isn't, and that's the one question you avoid like death" (*FB*, 28).

Nick has made his sudden departure because of a note he received from Rooney. She has gone to a small town called Muscadine, as Nick eventually discovers, to see a spiritual counselor, a strange woman named Lillian Flagg, because she can no longer bear alone the guilt arising from a single sexual encounter with Will Poteat, who has been spreading rumors about Rooney and Nick in his column. Lillian Flagg manages to help them both. Rooney returns to Myron. Nick makes a detour to visit his hypochondriac father, and while at his father's house has a moving and enigmatic experience of God that reveals the shape of Nick's faith. He then returns to Myron to find that Will has succeeded in stirring up the town's suspicions.

In the end Irma Reinwasser, a Jew, takes the blame and the sin of this small-town world upon herself, as did a Jew long ago. A modicum of redemption takes place around Irma's death. The circle of reconciliation at last includes even Will Poteat. And life goes on. In the pattern of Nick's experience—the children, the church and town, the deep-running stream of humor, Nick as saint and clown, "Harold be thy name," who runs a dancing school for angels, and the tragedy that is real but never the final word—the shape of his faith, perhaps even the shape of God, can be discerned.

In the next chapter I shall relate Buechner's publications to his developing career as a minister. Suffice it here to say that he left his post at Phillips Exeter Academy two years after *The Final Beast* appeared in 1965, and devoted himself to writing full-time. From his many sermons and meditations given before gatherings of the "cultured despisers of religion" making up his congregation at Exeter, he selected some for publication—*The Magnificent Defeat* in 1966 and *The Hungering Dark* in 1969.

The Magnificent Defeat is dedicated to James Muilenburg, his professor at Union Seminary who had influenced him so deeply. The same superb style and brilliant use of image and metaphor found in his novels appear here also. And the personal longing for faith and God that emerges in his fiction pours out directly with a compelling intensity. When he speaks of Jacob wrestling with the angel or Pope Pius XII searching the faces on either side of him as he is borne toward the altar at St. Peter's in Rome for a Christmas Eve mass, we are brought into the presence and the experience of Jacob and then of the pope by the vividness of Buechner's narrative.

In this book also there is a passage that throws light on an important aspect of Buechner's writing: the way he makes use of his own experience. He takes things that have happened to him and uses them in transmuted form, sometimes easily recognizable, sometimes not. In *The Magnificent Defeat* we find this passage in "The Shepherd" who comes to visit the infant Jesus:

"Night was coming on, and it was cold," the shepherd said, "and I was terribly hungry. I had finished all the bread I had in my sack, and my gut still ached for more. Then I noticed my friend, a shepherd like me, about to throw away a crust he didn't want. So I said, 'Throw the crust to me, friend!' and he did throw it to me, but it landed between us in the mud where the sheep had mucked it up. But I grabbed it anyway and stuffed it, mud and all, into my mouth. And as I was eating it, I suddenly saw—myself. It was as if I was not only a man eating but a man watching the man eating. And I thought, 'This is who I am. I am a man who eats muddy bread.' And I thought, 'The bread is very good.' And I thought, 'Ah, and the mud is very good too.' So I opened my muddy man's mouth full of bread, and I yelled to my friends, 'By God, it's good, brothers!' And they thought I was a terrible fool, but they saw what I meant. We saw everything that night, everything. Everything!" (*MD*, 71–72)

In *The Sacred Journey* he recounts an experience that happened to him years ago when he was in the Army that was to become, in changed form, something that happened to a shepherd even longer ago:

The next winter I sat in Army fatigues somewhere near Anniston, Alabama, eating my supper out of a mess kit. The infantry training battalion that I had been assigned to was on bivouac. There was a cold drizzle of rain, and everything was mud. The sun had gone down. I was still hungry when I finished eating and noticed that a man nearby had something left over that he was not going to eat. It was a turnip, and when I asked him if I could have it, he tossed it over to me. I missed the catch, the turnip fell to the ground, but I wanted it so badly that I picked it up and started eating it anyway, mud and all. And then, as I ate it, time deepened and slowed down again. With a lurch of the heart that is real to me still, I saw suddenly, almost as if from beyond time altogether, that not only was the turnip good, but the mud was good too, even the drizzle and cold were good, even the Army that I had dreaded for months. Sitting there in the Alabama winter with my mouth full of cold turnip and mud, I could see at least for a moment how if you ever took truly to heart the ultimate goodness and joy of things, even at their bleakest, the need to praise someone or something for it would be so great that you might even have to go out and speak of it to the birds of the air. (*SJ*, 85)

The Hungering Dark is dedicated to his former students and colleagues at the Phillips Exeter Academy. It contains another offering of sensitive and passionate witnesses to Buechner's faith, showing the sure hand of the novelist and theologian at work. In it also is another illustration of the way ideas from one part of his work appear in changed form elsewhere. In *The Hungering Dark* he writes, "To live for yourself alone, hoarding your life for your own sake, is in almost every sense that matters to reduce your life to a life hardly worth the living, and thus to lose it" (*HD*, 86). In *Open Heart* we find Leo Bebb describing his assistant, Brownie, in earthier terms: "He's played it so safe all his life he's never lived. He's slid his life in under his tail and sat on it. The man's got spiritual hemorrhoids" (*OH, BB*, 231).

In *The Entrance to Porlock* Buechner makes explicit an element in his writing that earlier had appeared around the edges or sometimes as pervasive atmosphere. It is the element of fairy tale. He introduces this dimension in *Porlock* by basing the novel on *The Wizard of Oz*, by patterning the main characters and the enveloping action on Baum's story, and by employing a style that interweaves fantasy with a continuing sense of reality.

Peter Ringkoping has converted a barn on a large tract of land on a small New England mountain into a bookstore, where he sells old and rare books, and where he periodically sees ghosts. Now entering his eighties, Peter has decided to give most of the land to a school for retarded adults run by Hans Strasser, who had once lived near the Ringkopings. The main action of the story emerges from the trip Peter, his two sons, his grandson, his wife, and his daughter-in-law make to Hans Strasser's school to arrange the gift.

Peter not only sees ghosts, he relates to other people in a ghostlike way and is better at quoting Shakespeare to his family than being a father to his sons or a husband to his wife. He is the Tin Woodman seeking a heart. Tommy, Peter's oldest son, married a woman with a little money and, coated with a protective layer of buffoonery, has settled in to a life of doing nothing. He is the Scarecrow seeking a brain. The second son, Nels, long-time dean at a boys secondary school, has recently been passed over in favor of an outsider for the post of headmaster. Deathly afraid of dying and constantly visualizing his own demise, he hides his fears and insecurities behind a facade of bluster. He is the Cowardly Lion in search of courage. Tip, the grandson, is trying to shape an identity for himself and, like Dorothy, is seeking a way home, if he can find where home is. The highway they take in order to get to the school for retarded adults is the Yellow Brick Road, and Pilgrim Village, the school itself, is the Emerald City. Hans Strasser, depicted as a kind of magician, is the Wizard.

This fairy-tale pattern, however, and the use of characters who parallel those in the fairy tale in no way inhibits Buechner's way with words or lively storytelling ability. *The Entrance to Porlock* is a powerful story in its own right, not a copy of *The Wizard of Oz*.

THE EXPLICIT SHAPE

After finishing *Porlock* Buechner faced a crisis in his sense of direction and vocation that we shall examine more carefully in the following chapter. It was just at his moment of near despair that he was asked to give the Noble Lectures at Harvard. Preparing what was eventually published as *The Alphabet of Grace* proved a turning point for Buechner. "What I started trying to do as a writer and as a preacher," he says, "was more and more to draw on my own experience not just as a source of plot, character, illustration, but as a source of truth" (*NT,* 87). As he worked through the gutturals, sibilants, and absence of vowels making up the story of his life, he discovered in it a language of grace by means of which he could speak to others. It gave him the courage to expose himself in his writings. And so he began this book with a note to the reader in which he confessed who he was: "I am a part-time novelist who happens also to be a part-time Christian . . . . Any Christian who is not a hero, Léon Bloy wrote, is a pig . . . . From time to time I find a kind of heroism momentarily possible — a seeing, doing, telling of Christly truth — but most of the time I am indistinguishable from the rest of the herd that jostles and snuffles at the great trough of life. Part-time novelist, Christian, pig. That is who I am" (*AG,* vii–viii).

His discovery of his own life as the best source for what he wished to say as writer and as minister was liberating for him. It let Leo Bebb emerge from that depth within Buechner that dreams come from and launched him on the most creative period of his life to date.

Buechner's next novel was *Lion Country,* which opens the series of four books about Leo Bebb. Bebb took hold of Buechner and would not let him go; *Open Heart* followed, then *Love Feast,* and then *Treasure Hunt.* The most prominent aspect of these novels is Bebb himself and the richness of characters and events around him. Buechner reports that the books almost wrote themselves.

Though each of the four has its own moments that for me are unforgettable, the first of these amazing stories is, I think, my favorite. *Lion Country* begins with Antonio Parr, who is in his mid-thirties, at loose ends in New York, visiting his twin sister, Miriam, who is dying of cancer. To pass the time and give his life a bit of meaning, he decides to write an exposé of a shady evangelist, Leo Bebb, who runs the Church of Holy Love and a religious diploma mill in Armadillo, Florida. Bebb apparently had been jailed earlier for exposing himself to some children at a Miami playground. Antonio goes to visit Bebb to get material, falls for Bebb's daughter Sharon, falls in another way for Bebb, and eventually finds himself family member, confidant, and skeptical disciple of Bebb. For Antonio, Bebb means life in an existence filled with death.

At one point Antonio meets Miriam's divorced husband, Charlie Blaine, to get Chris, twelve, and Tony, ten, Charlie and Miriam's children, and take them to the hospital. Charlie declines to go with them on what will probably be their last visit with their mother. "'I'll tell you how it is with me, Tono,' and his faded blue eyes took on a faraway look as though he was remembering some old script he had worked on for educational TV. 'I'd like to go up there with you in many ways, but in another way I'd rather not. You see, I prefer to remember her the way she was.'" And a few moments later, he adds, "'The truth of it is . . . . I'd be scared to death to go'" (*LC,* in *BB,* 84).

> I felt suddenly so sorry for him that I reached out and put my hand on his shoulder. I said, "Well, Charlie, don't take it too hard. I didn't mean to put you on the spot. Everybody's scared to death of something, and you just happen to be scared to death of death. For me it's life." (*LC* in *BB,* 84–85)

In spite of exposing whatever he had to expose in the past and for all his being just maybe a charlatan, Bebb helps Antonio and lots of others not to be afraid of life and even to come alive in their living. His trick eyelid that keeps winking in the midst of his most serious statements keeps us all guessing about Leo. One of the people he brings new life to is an old, oil-wealthy Indian from Texas named Herman Redpath. Herman, with much of the tribe he heads, comes to Armadillo to take part in a special service at the Church of Holy Love, in which Bebb restores the old Indian's sexual potency. During the ceremony, as Bebb is raising his arms in blessing, his robe opens down the front, exposing— well, the accounts differ as to details. Pandemonium breaks loose. Bebb fears the police will arrest him and send him back to prison. But, miraculously, Herman Redpath's potency is restored, and he invites Bebb, wife Lucille, daughter Sharon, and assistant Brownie to move to his ranch in Texas and run the Holy Love operation from there.

Bebb says it is like "when Moses led his people out of bondage in Egypt, the Lord opened up a path for them right through the Red Sea" (*LC* in *BB*, 120). And Bebb leads his people to the Redpath Ranch. Antonio returns to New York to be with Miriam through her death and her burial on Christmas Eve. The day after Christmas his loneliness overcomes him. He calls Bebb in Texas and arranges to fly there for a visit, finds Bebb comfortably settled, listens to Herman Redpath's obscene and funny monologues praising Bebb, and asks Sharon to marry him. They settle in Connecticut. Antonio resumes teaching in a high school. And Miriam's two boys come to live with them.

Lion Country ends with Antonio's reflection on Miriam's death and on his own living and dying:

> At my best and bravest I do not want to escape the future either, even though I know that it contains what will someday be my own great and final pain. Because a distaste for dying is twin to a taste for living, and again I don't think you can tamper with one without somehow doing mischief to the other. But this is at my best and bravest. The rest of the time I am a fool and a coward just like most of the other lost persons that in the end it will take no less than Mr. Keen himself to trace. (*LC* in *BB*, 128)

Open Heart picks up the story several years later. Antonio and Sharon have a baby, mostly looked after by nephew Chris, now eighteen. Nephew Tony has turned from fat, sleepy ten-year-old to sixteen-year-old high school jock. Antonio teaches English and coaches track at the high school in the Connecticut town where they live.

Herman Redpath is dying, and Antonio has gone to Texas to be with Bebb. Bebb conducts the funeral, and the tribal ceremonies surrounding the corpse give Redpath a rocketlike sendoff to the happy hunting ground. In his will the old chief has left money to endow the Church of Holy Love and its mail-order activities and give Bebb, as Bebb tells it, "One hundred thousand is what it says. One hundred thousand dollars to my loyal friend and pastor, Leo Bebb" (*OH* in *BB*, 146). Bebb decides to leave Holy Love in Brownie's supervision, while he moves on to take the Gospel to the North. Everything seems to be turning up roses for Bebb.

If *Lion Country* tells of Bebb's bondage in the past and then of his escape via a path opened through the Red Sea courtesy of Herman Redpath, then it would appear that Antonio is now going to relate Bebb's entry into the promised land. Instead, *Open Heart* comes nearer to telling about a trek through the wilderness.

Bebb moves to Connecticut and starts the Church of the Open Heart, but it never really works. A mysterious figure named Golden appears out of Bebb's past to haunt him and his wife, Lucille, who becomes increasingly upset and depressed. "You hear him say open your heart?" she says one Sunday after Bebb's sermon. "If I opened my heart, you'd tell me Lucille, shut it up again. Bebb, if he was to open his heart, you'd think you was dreaming" (*OH* in *BB*, 175). To cap it all, Antonio's nephew Tony confesses to having sex with Sharon.

Not long after, Lucille disappears. Eventually they discover that she has returned to the house she and Bebb lived in on Herman Redpath's ranch. Antonio and Bebb fly down, but by the time they arrive she has committed suicide by cutting her wrists and letting the blood run out as she sat on the porch in a rocking chair listening to Brownie read from the Bible.

After the funeral Bebb moves into the attic at Antonio and Sharon's. Because things are working or not working out between them, their marriage has been getting shakier. Bebb decides to close down the even shakier Church of the Open Heart for the following summer and take Sharon and Antonio on a trip to Europe. On the boat going over, Bebb falls in love with a blue-haired, seventy-five-year-old widow, a theosophist who thinks she and Bebb met in Egypt in a previous incarnation. Bebb and Grace Conover become companions, and Antonio and Sharon manage to stay together.

Back in Texas, when Brownie has finished telling Bebb and Antonio how Lucille had died, Bebb

walked over to Herman Redpath's organ across the room from
where Brownie and I were sitting . . . . He pulled out several of the
stops and pushed in several others. He settled his hands down on
the keyboard and started by pressing out several vague, overstuffed
chords.

Then he sang,

> *"Ten thousand times ten thousand,*
> *In sparkling raiment bright,*
> *The armies of the ransomed saints*
> *Throng up the steeps of light."*

There was something about his singing voice that always
reminded me of the Gothic radios of my childhood — reedy, maybe
one tube a little loose, the amber light of the dial.

He sang,

> *"Tis finished, all is finished,*
> *Their fight with death and sin.*
> *Fling open wide the golden gates,*
> *And let the victors in."* (OH in *BB,* 243)

Victors? Maybe. But death, if not totally triumphant, somehow
seems more in control, and open heart, in Lucille's case, anyway,
means open veins. Perhaps there is an underlying message in the
wilderness of *Open Heart*. When all's found, then all's lost. Getting
out of bondage and falling heir to a goodly portion of what this world
has to offer only sets us up for real loss. When we discover that all is
lost, it becomes possible that we may be found.

Love Feast carries forward the bittersweet themes of the first two
Bebb stories. When Bebb, Sharon, and Antonio return home from
Europe, and part company with Gertrude Conover, they find that the
building housing the Church of the Open Heart has burned down.
Bebb returns to the Church of Holy Love and Gospel Faith College in
Texas, but finding that he really isn't needed there, he moves in with
Gertrude Conover in her mansion in Princeton. They travel around the
world a great deal, but Antonio knows that Bebb isn't happy wander-
ing through Gertrude's landscape.

In the meantime, Antonio's older nephew, Chris, has finished high
school, gone to Harvard, shifted his interest from acting to making
money, and is becoming so successful in that role that he rarely comes
home any more. The younger nephew, Tony, who had stumbled into

a sexual encounter with Sharon, has finished high school and, not having the grades for college, stayed around Sutton at loose ends. Eventually he moves into a rooming house, leaving Antonio and Sharon at
home with their young son, Bill. Their shaky marriage gets shakier.

After a particularly stormy quarrel, Antonio moves out. Their sep-
aration hits Bebb hard. When Gertrude asks him what's wrong, he tells
her he's homesick but he doesn't know what he's homesick for any
more than she does. She suggests he think about all the young people
at Princeton University who may be homesick. "You know," she tells
Antonio later, "it worked like magic. He said to me, 'Blessed art thou
among women, Gertrude Conover,' and right there in the front seat of
the Lincoln he blossomed like a rose" (*LF* in *BB*, 298). He decides they
should throw a Thanksgiving dinner and invite all the Princeton
undergraduates left on campus over the holiday.

They put posters announcing the dinner at strategic places on
campus and prepare food for hundreds. Only a few people sign up in
advance and, by one o'clock on Thanksgiving, barely a dozen have
shown up. Instead of settling for them, Bebb proposes that rather than
waste all that food they take a leaf from Jesus' story of the great feast,
go out on the streets, round up anybody they can find, and bring them
back. Antonio is dubious. "How did you invite people to a parable?"
he asks himself. "Whom did you invite" (*LF* in *BB*, 303)? But out he
goes along with the rest of them.

Somehow it works. From the highways and byways and hedges,
they bring in the oddest assortment of humanity imaginable. With
Bebb's leadership it turns into a great love feast, with people hugging
and singing and telling their stories. One woman named Nancy
Oglethorpe undergoes a real conversion, stands up and tells about the
life she has been leading and has decided to lead no more, and winds
up saying they ought to keep up what they've started. "I think," said
Nancy Oglethorpe, slowly sweeping the room with her glance, "I think
we should try to make Princeton, New Jersey, one big love feast for
Jesus" (*LF* in *BB*, 310). And they do.

Bebb sets out on a great new phase of his life, while Antonio
returns to his hell in smalltown Connecticut:

> Life must go on, so they say, and by the same token I suppose
> death also must go on, the two of them hand in hand like old play-
> mates. Life was Bebb, it seemed to me then — Bebb launched on a

brilliant new career with Nancy Oglethorpe and Gertrude Conover both beside him at the tiller, Bebb poised to evangelize Princeton, New Jersey, to set up the Supper of the Lamb in the groves of academe. And death was me returning to Mrs. Gunther's boarding house in Sutton, Connecticut, was me driving to school past the house where my wife and son lived as if I had died there. (*LF* in *BB,* 311)

Life and death are wrestling throughout the Bebb stories, as indeed they are contending with one another in Buechner's experience and in the experience of all of us, if we have awareness enough to notice or have been jolted into awareness by someone such as Bebb. In one perspective death wins in *Love Feast,* as indeed it eventually wins over us all.

For all their life-giving exuberance, the love feasts get thrown out of Princeton because a professor of history named Virgil Roebuck keeps after the university to get rid of them. Because of circumstances surrounding the closure and because the IRS is apparently after him about his failure to file proper returns, Bebb chooses to go underground. In the meantime, Antonio and Sharon get back together and have a baby girl. Bebb returns to Princeton on Reunion Day in a small plane with streamers behind it saying, Here's to Jesus and Here's to You. He also drops leaflets all over the town with Love is a Feast and a picture of himself on them. Afterward the plane crashes in a field, and, though the bodies of Bebb and his friend Clarence Golden, who was with him, are never found, the men are assumed to be dead.

Brownie and some of the Indians come up from Texas for Bebb's funeral. And Gertrude Conover provides his epitaph. "'Leo Bebb was always good company,' she said" (*LF* in *BB,* 398).

Treasure Hunt has an elusive, now-you-see-it, now-you-don't quality about it. At first glance it's a wild and weird goose chase to South Carolina, where Antonio, Sharon, and Gertrude get a glimpse of the world in which Leo Bebb grew up, and Sharon learns more about her own past than she had bargained for. If you look again, using the corners of your eyes carefully, you may see the post-Resurrection narrative in the Gospel according to Bebb. Paraphrasing Mark 16:7, we might say, "Tell his disciples that Bebb is going before you to Poinsett, South Carolina. There you will see him."

The story starts with them around Gertrude Conover's swimming pool listening to Bebb's voice on a tape:

It said, "The trouble with folks like Brownie is they hold their life in like a bakebean fart at a Baptist cookout and only let it slip out sideways a little at a time when they think there's nobody noticing. Now that's the last thing on earth the Almighty intended. He intended all the life a man's got inside him, he should live it out just as free and strong and natural as a bird. (*TH* in *BB*, 407)

That's Bebb, all right. And he winds up telling them what he wants them to do:

"There's a piece of land outside of Spartanburg, South Carolina, that belongs to me. It's down there in a place name of Poinsett that's where I was born and raised, and there's a house on it that's mine too. I don't suppose anybody's lived there going on twenty-five, thirty years, but far as I know it's still standing. It's the house I first saw the light of day in. Up to the day I got married and moved out, it was home . . . .
. . . "Antonio, I'm leaving that place to Sharon and you. The land and the old homestead. Both. I'm not laying anything on you what to do with it . . . . But you mind this.
. . . I want you to do something nice with that old place. And I want you to do it for Jesus." (*TH* in *BB*, 413)

How did Gertrude get the tape? It seems that Bebb had dropped in to visit her the previous week as she was sitting on the terrace in the late evening. He was very much alive ("the cosmic batteries can recharge very rapidly," she tells them) and not at all fuzzy around the edges. He chatted, ate several graham crackers, and told her she would find the tape under some things in his closet. It was there.

Though Antonio and Sharon have some misgivings, they set out on their journey with Gertrude and her chauffeur, Callaway, in her Lincoln to Poinsett (pronounced Points by the natives). Antonio persuades Brownie, who has lost his faith and hopes somehow to find it again, to join them in South Carolina. They find the house still standing, occupied by Bebb's twin brother, Babe, whom Bebb had never mentioned, and his wife, Bertha. Babe runs a museum called the Uforium, with evidences of visitors from outer space, and has stories as astounding as anything to be found in the Book of Revelation.

The revelations about Bebb unfold along the way, explaining

Babe's hostility toward him. Among other things, Bebb had gotten Bertha pregnant. Babe wouldn't have the child around, so Bebb and Lucille took it to replace their baby that had died. This offspring of Bebb and Bertha was Sharon.

By a mysterious process of her own, Gertrude decides that Bebb was reincarnated in a little blind boy born about the time of Bebb's death. Babe at first resists turning over the house to Sharon as Bebb's heir. After some stormy scenes he departs, and Bertha decides to go with him, with Sharon losing her mother again almost as soon as she has found her. Antonio and Sharon decide to let the family of little Jimmy Bob Luby, Bebb reincarnate, live in the house. They have too many children for the trailer they have been occupying, and they are too poor to get a better place on their own.

As they prepare to leave Poinsett to return home, Gertrude says, "Well, there is nothing nicer you could have done for Jesus than that," and as she waves good-bye to the blind, unknowing Jimmy Bob, she speaks to Bebb, "And I will love thee still, my dear, till a' the seas gang dry" (*TH* in *BB,* 527).

Sharon has found the treasure of knowing who she is, and Antonio, more reconciled to who he is, returns home with Sharon and comes nearer to knowing the place as home. At the end of it all he writes that he has tried to speak what he has felt in

> this account of my life and times, my own search, I suppose, for whatever it is we search for in Poinsett, South Carolina, and Sutton, Connecticut, for whatever it is that is always missing. I am not sure I have ever seen it even from afar, God knows, and I know I don't have forever to see it in either. Already, if I make the mistake of listening, I can hear a dim humming in the tracks, Time's wingéd chariot hurrying near, as Andrew Marvell said to his coy mistress. But to be honest I must say that on occasion I can also hear something else too — not the thundering of distant hoofs, maybe, or *Hi-yo, Silver. Away!* echoing across the lonely sage, but the faint chunk-chunk of my own moccasin heart, of the Tonto afoot in the dusk of me somewhere who, not because he ought to but because he can't help himself, whispers *Kemo Sabe* every once in a while to what may or may not be only a silvery trick of the failing light. (*TH* in *BB,* 530)

So the incredible Bebb chronicle ends but really doesn't end, because, like all good parables, especially those of Jesus, the story becomes woven into our own lives and opens us for a future in which Bebb and Sharon and Antonio and Brownie and Herman Redpath and Gertrude Conover, and maybe even the Lone Ranger and Tonto become, with Jesus, our companions on a way that sometimes makes sense if we can just remember that the worst things are never the last things. Here's to Jesus. Here's to you. Like Jesus and Bebb, may you always be good company.

The liberation that the Noble Lectures and Bebb brought to Buechner emerged in other books. *Wishful Thinking: A Theological ABC,* published in 1973, is a brief dictionary of theological terms, done with a pungency and wit that will awaken those too used to hearing them and attract those who reject them or have never heard them. For example, "An agnostic is somebody who doesn't know for sure whether there really is a God. That is some people all of the time and all people some of the time" (*WT,* 1). Or about feet. "Generally speaking, if you want to know who you really are as distinct from who you like to think you are, keep an eye on where your feet take you" (*WT,* 27). Written at the same time as he was making the acquaintance of Leo Bebb, this little book shows the greater spontaneity that Bebb gave Buechner.

Peculiar Treasures: A Biblical Who's Who, published in 1979, does the same thing for biblical figures that *Wishful Thinking* does for biblical and theological terms. Added to Buechner's insightful text are delightful illustrations by his daughter Katherine. Of Ahab, he writes, "Whereas just about everybody has a cross to bear, King Ahab had two. One cross was the prophet Elijah. If, generally speaking, a prophet to a king was like ants at a picnic, Elijah was like a swarm of bees. The other cross was his foreign-born wife, Jezebel, who had gotten religion in a big way back in the old country and was forever trying to palm it off on the Israelites" (*PT,* 9).

The Faces of Jesus (1974) is a marvelous collection of pictures of painting and sculpture depicting Jesus, with an accompanying text by Buechner. In the introduction he writes:

> So once again, for the last time or the first time, we face that face — all the ways humans have dreamed it down the years, painted and sculpted it, scratched it into the teeth of whales, stitched it into wool and silk, hammered it out of gold. There it is . . . . Like the

faces of the people we love, it has become so familiar that unless we take pains we hardly see it at all. Take pains. See it for what it is and, to see it whole, see it too for what it is just possible that it will become: the face of Jesus as the face of our own secret and innermost destiny:

The face of Jesus is our face. (*FJ,* 14)

Buechner's Lyman Beecher Lectures at Yale were published as *Telling the Truth: The Gospel as Tragedy, Comedy, and Fairy Tale* (1977). In beautiful and moving words, he talks about the truth that the Gospel is and how it takes all our experience of life's tragedies, all the comic powers we can muster, and all the imaginative sense of fairy tale we can bring to the task in order even to put a frame of words around the great silence that is the Gospel truth.

The next Buechner novel is the story of Godric. Though it reminds us of all that has gone before in Buechner's writing, this book must be viewed in a class unto itself among the novels. It is the story of a medieval saint, told in the first person from his perspective when he is older than one hundred and anticipating his death in the not-too-distant future. Godric still thinks of himself as a great sinner, which apparently he was in the first forty years of life before he became a hermit. But others think him a saint.

Godric is a strange book, as also is this most unsaintly saint. Its time and place and story seem so far from ours. Yet I find myself drawn to this contrary old figure and his strange-angle world.

The abbott of a nearby monastery has sent a young monk, Reginald, "to put your life on parchment, Godric" (*G,* 6). It is a trial for Godric to have Reginald constantly turning the old sinner into a great saint. More vividly even than Nicolet or Bebb, Godric is both. In memory, he holds the wholeness of his life before him and "deep inside this wrecked and ravaged hull, there sails a young man still . . . . So ever and again young Godric's dreams well up to flood old Godric's prayers, or prayers and dreams reach God in such a snarl he has to comb the tangle out, and who knows which he counts more dear" (*G,* 40).

We hear his life unfold from early days through success as a seafaring merchant, roistering, wenching, peddling, stealing, with adventures from England to the Holy Land. When he returns home grown into a man, he finds that his father has died and his mother is wasting away from grief. "The sadness was I'd lost a father I had never fully found. It's like a tune that ends before you've heard it out. Your whole life through you search to catch the strain, and seek the face you've lost in strangers' faces" (*G*, 51).

His mother asks him to join her on a pilgrimage to Rome. Later he makes a pilgrimage to Jerusalem. And around age forty, following a tugging that has long been in his heart, he becomes a hermit and lives beside the River Wear near Durham. In prayer and repentance he spends more than sixty years there, his heart filled with the sorrows of his life and the hope his faith in God gives him. Now this centenarian, with his amazingly varied life spread out before him, is burdened with a chronicler who does not want the vividly remembered truth of his life but rather will hear only what is good. Godric, who knows himself as a great sinner, is regarded unwaveringly by his pious biographer as a great holy man. Tiresomely, Reginald launders everything Godric says and does until it fits the saint's story that he is determined to write. As I am drawn into Godric's long-gone world, it tells me much about my own experience and world.

Reginald says of Godric's end, "When death came for him at last, he did not quail before it but suffered it to bear him off as easily as a river bears off a fallen leaf" (*G*, 175). Godric, undoubtedly, would give us a saltier and truer account of his dying than Reginald's pious version.

Buechner's next publications were his two volumes of autobiography: *The Sacred Journey* (1982) and *Now and Then* (1983). Both are sensitively written accounts of the events in his life that, in his perspective, have shaped him and his art. In a very real sense, learning that his most important resource was his own experience and then, with the help of Bebb, getting the courage to expose himself to public view made the writing of these volumes possible. And, in another way, the practice Buechner had already had in writing *The Alphabet of Grace*, the Bebb novels, and *Godric* enabled him to deal with autobiographical materials in a way that made them as interesting as novels. Not only does the Good News that is the Gospel need tragedy, comedy, and fairy tale to do its truth justice, so also does the news that is one's life story need all three.

Except for the newly released *Whistling in the Dark* (1988), Buechner's most recent book of nonfiction, published in 1984, is *A Room Called Remember: Uncollected Pieces*. In the preface he writes, "Best to be honest about it—the book is a grab bag. There are a handful of sermons preached at places like Harvard, the Pacific School of Religion, the Congregational Church of Rupert, Vermont, and one that has never been preached anywhere at all, . . ." some articles, "a commencement address, . . . a lecture on 'The Speaking and Writing of Words,' . . . and a short autobiographical piece" for the *Christian Century (RCR,* ix).

In a sense there is a grab-bag quality about all Buechner's writing. I do not mean that the contents of each book are miscellaneous and lacking connectedness. Rather, I intend the more complimentary judgment that Buechner's writings exhibit an artful spontaneity and demonstrate his ability to bring the diversity of ordinary human experience, specifically *his* ordinary human experience, into focus upon the God of biblical faith, and do it in ways that amaze, entertain, and, mayhap, touch the human heart of readers and hearers for good.

Who will Buechner produce as characters in his next novel? The central figure is Brendan the Navigator, a sixth-century Irish saint. Whatever happens to Brendan, we can be sure he will reach out to us as Buechner probes new depths of human experience.

The world as Buechner depicts it is a mixture—pain and pleasure, evil and good, suffering and joy, hate and love. Through Christian experience and faith, the shape of God has the twisted look of one crucified. Yet the hope is there amid the pain, and ever humming through it all is a rumble of divine and human laughter. Though all may seem lost, we find through the greatest cosmic joke of all that all at last is found.

CHAPTER 4

Portrait of the Artist

"At its heart most theology, like most fiction, is essentially autobiography," Buechner says. And he adds, "Like most theology, most fiction is of course also at its heart autobiography" (*AG,* 3, 7). By no means should this be taken to imply that Buechner merely makes his own life story the subject of all his art and his theology. It is equally clear, however, that he and his own story are never absent from his writing. Perhaps the way to put it best is that Buechner provides living demonstration that both theology and fiction must, if they are to mean anything at all to the writer or to the reader, be grounded in the author's own sacred, human journey.

Out of his life experience, Buechner writes consciously as a Christian, but not as a propagandist for the church. There are too many doubts and difficulties that go into the makeup of his faith to permit any facile proclamation of assured dogmas. Of his novels, Buechner says, "I don't start with some theological axe to grind, but with a deep, wordless feeling for some aspect of my own experience that has moved me" (*NT,* 59). From there the characters emerge and the plot takes shape, yet the element of confession remains central.

What I find in his work are the dimensions of astonishment and perplexity that are common to us all. Within this context his writing, then, becomes a mirror in which all of us may see the varied faces of our own lives and relationships, and a window through which we can see, with artful prodding from Buechner, that there "is no event so commonplace but that God is present within it" (*NT,* 87).

In this chapter I shall look at Buechner's background, experience, and development. This is not a biography or even a biographical sketch. It is more like a painting, with elements selected that enable us to visualize the person behind the words, so I call it a portrait of the artist.

In addition to giving information about his life, I shall also show the close relation between what has happened to him and what he has written. Just as I told of my first encounters with Buechner's writing in the introduction and tried to delineate the shape of his work in Chapter 3, so now it will be possible to relate his books to the stages of his life journey. By examining his roots we can see that Buechner's writing grows out of who he has been and is becoming. Even more, by looking at the course his life has taken, we can understand better how he has evolved into an artist with his own special insight and power.

EARLY LIFE: REALITY AS KALEIDOSCOPE

Buechner is pronounced Beekner, he tells us. "If somebody mispronounces it in some foolish way, I have the feeling that what's foolish is me. If somebody forgets it, I feel that it's I who am forgotten. There's something about it that embarrasses me in just the same way that there's something about me that embarrasses me" (*WT,* 12.) This feeling about his name takes shape and meaning in the light of the insecurities that plagued his early life.

He was born in New York City on July 11, 1926. On both sides of the family, there was wealth and social status. The relationships and expectations of this background were present in his immediate family, but not the money. His father shifted from one position to another in search of a success that eluded him as persistently as he continued to demand substantial achievement from himself.

One consequence of moving from place to place was a feeling of homelessness for the mother and two young sons, as well as for the father. "I suppose it was having no one house I had lived in always that made the world seem so perilous and uncertain," Buechner suggests.

> Virtually every year of my life until I was fourteen, I lived in a different place, had different people to take care of me, went to a different school. The only house that remained constant was the one where my maternal grandparents lived in a suburb of Pittsburgh called East Liberty. . . . Apart from that one house on Woodland Road, home was not a place to me when I was a child. It was people. (*SJ,* 19–21)

In the fall of 1936, when Buechner was ten years old, his father committed suicide, the result, apparently, of thinking himself a complete failure. It was a Saturday morning. The father looked in on his sons playing in their room with a roulette wheel. Then he went down to the garage, started the automobile motor, and let the carbon monoxide fumes kill him. The boys, told to stay in their room, looked down from the window on the scene as their mother and grandmother brought their father out into the driveway and attempted to revive him. They saw the doctor come, examine the body, and shake his head. "It was not for several days that a note was found. It was written in pencil on the last page of *Gone with the Wind*, which had been published that year, 1936, and it was addressed to my mother. 'I adore and love you,' it said, 'and am no good. . . . Give Freddy my watch. Give Jamie my pearl pin. I give you all my love'" (*SJ*, 41).

In and through these experiences that were shredding the foundations of his security, the artist was already emerging. After his father's death his mother moved them to Bermuda. Buechner calls it the Land of Oz, and preparation for living in that enchanted country had begun long before, during those years of homeless wandering.

> It was in Washington too that at this same time I was sick for the better part of a year with a glittering combination of pneumonia, tonsillitis, and pleurisy, and during the period that I was in bed, I lived, as much as I could be said to live anywhere, not in the United States of America but in the Land of Oz. One Oz book after another I read or had read to me until the world where animals can speak, and magic is common as grass, and no one dies, was so much more real to me than the world of my own room that if I had had occasion to be homesick then, it would have been Oz, not home, that I would have been homesick for as in a way I am homesick for it still. (*SJ*, 14–15)

So Oz and the house of his maternal grandparents near Pittsburgh provided stability through the changes of his childhood. He is probably correct, however, that it was not the place but the people that were most important. And one person in particular, his maternal grandmother, was paramount.

Both his grandmothers were strong. "Grandma Buechner was a rock," too stolid for the imaginative youngster (*SJ*, 31). She lived in

New York. It was instead the unruffled, mysterious, and bewitching Grandmother Kuhn, whom he called Naya, who shored up the shaking foundations of his life; "of all the giants who held up my world," he writes, "Naya was perhaps chief" (*SJ*, 31). She played a crucial role for him, not only when she lived in Pittsburgh, but also later, when he, his brother, and their mother lived with the Kuhn grandparents in Tryon, North Carolina. His beautiful dedication of *A Long Day's Dying* and his references in *The Alphabet of Grace* make his debt to Naya clear.

Through all the shifting scenes in these early years, that embryonic artist in him developed, nourished first by pictures, which made him want to become a painter, then by his passion for reading and the vivid terrain into which books drew him, and, most of all, by his love of words and his discovery of "the great power that language has to move and in some measure even to transform the human heart" (*SJ*, 69).

STARTING POINT: SUCCESS AND DISAPPOINTMENT

He attended Lawrenceville School in New Jersey and then went on to Princeton University. His studies at Princeton were interrupted by a tour of duty in the army, in Alabama. After being discharged he returned to Princeton to complete his undergraduate education, still filled with an overwhelming sense of meaninglessness. But now something else was happening to him.

> *Beyond time* is the phrase that I have used to describe this leg of my journey because it was then that I think I first began to have a pale version of the experience that Saint Paul describes in his letter to the Philippians. "Work out your own salvation with fear and trembling," he writes, "for God is at work in you both to will and to work for his good pleasure." I was a long way from thinking in terms of my own salvation or anybody else's, but through the people I met . . . through my revulsion at my own weaknesses as well as through such satisfaction as I had in my own strengths, it seems to me now that a power from beyond time was working to achieve its own aim through my aimless life in time as it works through the lives of all of us and all our times. (*SJ*, 94–95)

The kaleidoscopic character of his early experience was beginning to acquire more stable form. The parts of the picture were coming into focus. And an important sign of the change was that in his senior year at Princeton he began writing a novel.

The process that had begun in the class taught by Mr. Martin at Lawrenceville School, where, incidentally, Thornton Wilder had taught in the 1920s, and continued with his study at Princeton with R. P. Blackmur was coming to fruition. And so he began work on his first novel and completed it during the first year after graduation, while he was teaching creative writing at Lawrenceville.

A Long Day's Dying was published in January 1950, when Buechner was only twenty-three years old. The novel was highly acclaimed and, as Buechner notes, it "turned out unaccountably to be a best-seller" (*SJ*, 99). He found himself compared to Henry James and Marcel Proust. There was no doubt that he had shown himself, in his first major publication, to be a superb writer, though it was equally apparent that he felt uncertain that he had anything to say worth saying. Retrospectively, he regarded his motive for writing in those early days as seeking glory rather than believing that he had any significant content to communicate. He wanted recognition, yet at the same time he had deep feelings of ambivalence about his success.

In any event, he managed to get through his moment in the public eye unscathed. And his second novel, *The Seasons' Difference*, published in 1952, was as highly *un*acclaimed as the first had been praised, so the problem of too much success soon disappeared. Instead, the failure proved to be almost more than his fragile, emerging sense of purpose could withstand.

TURNING POINT: THE FACE OF THE MYSTERY BECOMES THE FACE OF CHRIST

Just when the aimlessness of his life was being overcome, the bottom dropped out. The success of the first novel was not sufficient to compensate for the failure that followed. He found it difficult to write. As he expressed it in a letter, "I did not take a job though I considered the possibility—the advertising business, the *New Yorker* magazine, the CIA. I kept on trying to write and seeing a lot of a girl I was in love with." Among other things, he also started going to church. Thus it happened that, while living on the upper East Side of Manhattan, he was somehow led to the Presbyterian church where George Buttrick was the preacher and into that dramatic experience of conversion "among confession, and tears, and great laughter" that I told about earlier.

At a time in his life when, in various ways, Buechner felt empty and lost, he was seeking and, though he admits discomfort with putting it this way, found Christ—or was found by him. If we are to call Buechner a novelist/theologian of the lost and found, then it is important for us to know that he is the one who, first and foremost in his experience, was lost and then, in unlikely but still unforgettable circumstances, was found.

> To say that I was born again, to use that traditional phrase, is to say too much because I remained in most ways as self-centered and squeamish after the fact as I was before, and God knows remain so still. And in another way to say that I was born again is to say too little because there have been more than a few such moments since, times when from beyond time something too precious to tell has glinted in the dusk, always just out of reach, like fireflies. (*SJ*, 111)

As a result of the experience he had while listening to Buttrick's sermon, Buechner went to talk with the great preacher about going to seminary. Buttrick took him seriously enough to escort him personally to Union Theological Seminary on the upper West Side of New York and introduce him to people there who could advise him on how to enroll. And so, from the church on Madison Avenue, his journey took him to an exploration of Christian faith in a divinity school.

What is important for us here in seeking to understand Buechner is that his life, already focused on writing, now began to acquire significant content about which to write. But it was a process that took time.

At Union he encountered the theologians and biblical scholars who became his mentors, not only by what they said but by who they were. Buechner mentions several of his teachers in particular. There was Reinhold Niebuhr, who "had a nose quick to sniff out the irony and ambivalence of things in general and of piety in particular" (*NT*, 13). Paul Tillich, he says, had a vivid sense of the "here and there," "now and then," "usually hidden" way the New Creation manifests itself. Most of all, there was James Muilenburg, who "*was* the Old Testament," a fool for Christ "in the sense that he didn't or couldn't or wouldn't resolve, intellectualize, evade, the tensions of his faith but lived those tensions out, torn almost in two by them at times" (*NT,* 15, 16).

These theological giants helped Buechner shape his own faith and discipline his passion. But it was Muilenburg more than any of the others who, by daring in class to act out the apostacies, battles, and blessings of the biblical figures, gave Buechner a sense of the incarnational nature of faith and enabled him to embark on the way toward the freedom to express it artistically in wild and wonderful ways. The main reason probably that Leo Bebb and the fantastic array of characters that surrounded him in the Bebb novels could emerge in Buechner's imagination and be permitted their release into public view was because of the far horizons of faith into which he was led by Muilenburg.

While attending seminary Buechner happened to go to a family gathering. There he met the woman he eventually married—Judith Merck. It was, he says, an accident of grace. After all, suppose he hadn't gone!

Though his world was expanding and undergoing drastic changes, Buechner continued to write during his time at Union. The novel he completed during this time was very different from his earlier ones, though a far cry from those he would eventually create. *The Return of Ansel Gibbs,* with the government and the mass media as background, begins to include the theological and social perspectives Buechner is acquiring in seminary. Of special significance is the character patterned after James Muilenburg. In this book also, Buechner is able to begin dealing, in fictional form at least, with the suicide of his father. What he had lost and repressed in his own life was, with pain and turmoil, beginning to be found.

CRUCIBLE: THE SEASONING'S DIFFERENCE

With the end of his seminary education near, Buechner found himself wrestling with the problem of what it would mean for him to become pastor of a congregation. There was no doubt in his mind about being committed to some form of Christian ministry. He writes:

> What I wanted above all else was to try to bring the Christian faith to life in all its richness and depth for others the way people like Buttrick, Muilenburg, Tillich, and the rest had brought it to

life for me, and for that reason what I needed more than anything else, I thought, was a pulpit. So if I could find a church that would have me, that was where I was prepared to go. As graduation from Union approached, I can't remember having even imagined any other possibility. (*NT,* 41)

The problem was that he had grown up in a nonchurchgoing family and, therefore, knew little about what went on in the average parish church. But, so far as he knew, being a minister meant having a church.

It meant conducting not just the services on Sundays, but the baptisms, the weddings, the funerals on whatever days they happened to turn up. It meant presiding over Sunday School and youth fellowships and other such groups. . . . Having a church meant calling on sick people in hospitals and on the old, the lonely, the house-bound who had no one else much to call on them. It meant worrying about budgets and fund drives, committees and trustees. (*NT,* 40)

Three years of seminary had done little to prepare him for the world of the local church. Becoming a minister in that sense was threatening for him because he feared he would be incompetent.

Fortunately, an attractive alternative presented itself. Robert Russell Wicks, dean of the chapel at Princeton when Buechner was in college there and later a colleague on the faculty at Lawrenceville, was, in his busy retirement years, serving as school minister at Phillips Exeter Academy and trying to organize a program of religious instruction there. He wrote Buechner, offering him a job teaching. Buechner thought it over carefully and accepted. It seemed an excellent way to carry out his call to Christian ministry without entering the unknown world of the local church.

"At Exeter," he writes, ". . . I would have the chance to set up some rigorous, academically respectable courses in the subject [of religion] and to try to establish them as an enterprise no less serious, relevant, and demanding than the study of American history or physics. Even though it was not a form of ministry that I had ever considered, I decided to give it a try" (*NT,* 43).

And so he was ordained into the Presbyterian ministry, not as a minister who would be serving a congregation, but as a minister without pastoral charge, or, as it was stated, an "evangelist." Speaking at his ordination service were James Muilenburg and John Knox, his Old and New Testament professors at Union Seminary.

Buechner arrived at Exeter in September 1958, with a pregnant wife and no clear idea of what to expect in this new career on which he was embarked. The combination of vocational purposes that brought him to the school and the challenges he faced there proved a fateful mix. Exeter was the crucible that produced the novelist/theologian.

What he did not know when he arrived, but discovered early, was that he had to engage in a running battle with a student body and a faculty that was sophisticated, cynical, and, for the most part, antireligious. The students were anti just about everything, "anti-government, anti-establishment, anti-God, and anti-authority in any form whatsoever. As intellectuals, their heroes, if they admitted to having any, were people like Jack Kerouac, Allen Ginsberg, Jules Feiffer, Bertrand Russell, Sartre, and Ayn Rand." Religion as they found it was a special object of opposition.

> When it came to the Christian church in particular, and more particularly still when it came to the school church, which, whether they believed in God or didn't, all students were required to attend on Sundays unless they chose a town church instead, their opposition was boundless and impassioned. It was the final outrage perpetrated upon them by the combined authority of school, parents, establishment, and the very God they wouldn't touch with a ten-foot pole even if it could be proved to them that God existed. (NT, 44)

As the only teacher in the new religion department, Buechner became the focus of students' efforts to discredit and reject the faith they were convinced was wrong. He was fighting a war, as Buechner saw it, "to convince as many as I could that religious faith, even if they chose to have none of it, was not as bankrupt and banal and easily disposable as they most of them believed. It was a war to prove not just to my students but to certain equally skeptical members of the faculty and administration that religion both could and should be taught at all" (NT, 45).

The challenge was constant and difficult, and Buechner rose to meet it. His work in the classroom confirmed his own faith and strengthened his sense of purpose that what he was doing was eminently worthwhile. Then, to this already tremendous task of teaching, another was added—that of preaching.

> After Dean Wicks' final retirement, I became the school minister as well as the chairman of the religion department, and although I followed the tradition of getting visiting ministers to preach at the school church two or three Sundays out of each month—the most varied and effective ones I could find—at least one Sunday a month the job was mine, and I can still remember the sheer terror of it. They were so bright, those three hundred-odd boys, in some cases so much more so, I was afraid, than I was myself. And they were so literate. And, worse still, most if not all of them were there so much against both their wills and their principles, with somebody from the dean's office to check attendance and to wreak terrible vengeance on them if they were absent or late. There were also, in addition to the few faculty members who came regularly because they wanted to, others of them who came every once in a while because they felt they ought to or simply out of curiosity. They were often jaded, skeptical, sometimes even quite openly negative about the whole religious enterprise, but I was their friend and colleague, after all, and I suppose they thought there was always the off-chance that someday I might say something worth hearing. All in all, it was a sobering group to face on a Sunday morning. (*NT*, 67–68)

Not only did Buechner confront the challenge; he met and surmounted it over the next few years. He also enjoyed the sheer excitement and daring of preaching and teaching. The demanding context into which he had been thrust compelled him to draw on all his skill with words and all the resources he had accumulated at Union and beyond. Even more, the situation of white-hot battle forged the bonding of art and faith that began to shape his perspective and his writing. In a significant way, a new Buechner emerged from his struggles on the academic fields of Exeter.

> I wrote my sermons at great length and with great care. I learned to write in shorter, simpler sentences than I had in my books because a listener loses track otherwise. Though I never

dared step into the pulpit without everything, including the Lord's Prayer and the announcements, fully written out in front of me, I learned to be free enough of my manuscript to be able to read it without appearing to do so. I put on the best performance I could, in other words, and preached with all the eloquence I could muster, not only to them, of course, but also to myself because much of what preachers say they say always to themselves, to keep their own spirits up, to answer their own souls' questions—the sermon as whistling in the dark. There were times when I felt that something better and truer than my words was speaking through my words. There were times when I felt they were only words. There were times when the words seemed to fall dead from my lips and other times when I could see only too clearly how effective they were being. And maybe I entirely misjudged which time was which. I don't know. I know only that Barth is surely right when he says that no one risks the wrath of God more perilously than the minister in the pulpit, and yet at the same time I know that, as a minister, there are few places I would rather be. The excitement and challenge of it. The chance that something better than what you are can happen, that something more than you know can be spoken and heard. (NT, 70–71)

In spite of the personal satisfaction and success that he found in his work at Exeter, he neither could nor wanted to give up his calling to be a writer. In part he fulfilled this vocation through the sermons, many of which would later be published in the books of meditations. But the theological novelist as well as the artistic theologian were taking shape within him and continued to struggle for expression.

VOCATION: THE MEANING OF HIS MINISTRY

After almost five years at Exeter, Buechner took a sabbatical. For fifteen months he and his family lived on their farm in Vermont and he used the time for work on a fourth novel. The result was *The Final Beast*. This was his first novel written after he had completed seminary and been ordained. It was also the first after his seasoning as teacher and preacher. The book reflects, in transmuted form, his experience at Exeter and, above all, expresses the joy and the pain he had discovered in ministry.

In this novel Buechner found the style that enabled him to combine in an integral way his call to the ministry and his call to be a writer. He discovered in *The Final Beast* how to deal seriously with Christian faith in and through the struggles of human living. The comic and tragic are woven together in the interaction of characters that have both the smell of reality about them and the ambience of a fairy tale. He succeeded in shaping that creative fusion of theology and art that characterize his fiction from that time forward.

With the sabbatical and the novel finished, Buechner returned to the ministry at Exeter. But the time away devoted to writing, and also the growing conviction that he had at last found the way to unite theology and art, gave him a new perspective on the shape his ministry must take in the future. In the spring of 1967, almost nine years after coming to Exeter, Buechner made one of the most difficult decisions of his life — to resign his position at the school and move to the farm in Vermont, where he would develop his ministry through his writing.

The move was not made without many doubts and ambivalent feelings. On the one hand, he felt he had done a good job at Exeter. The religious studies program was going well. Student attitudes had shifted from the negativism toward religion characteristic when he came in 1958 to the student activism of the 1960s. On the other hand, there was no longer the challenge of the early years to develop a respectable religion department from scratch and win a place for Christian faith in a hostile environment. All in all, he decided, it was time to move on.

There was no question for either Judy or me about Vermont being the place we wanted to live, and we both loved the idea of being there all year round for awhile, watching the seasons change and not having to pack up and leave every September. But I had considerable misgivings about it, too. I was giving up a good job and burning my bridges behind me. I had a novel I wanted to write, but there is never any assurance that the words will flow when you want them to. And even if they did, was the writing of novels a fitting occupation for a minister anyway? Was I just leaving the comfortableness of Exeter for a life more comfortable still? Would I be writing for the glory of God or just for my own glory? To look at it another way, I would be on my own with no institution, no colleagues, to draw support from, with no bells ringing to remind me of my responsibilities, no structure to my life other than whatever structure I found it possible to impose on it myself. But we had decided to go, and go we did. (*NT,* 75–76)

Once settled on the farm in Vermont, Buechner began work on his fifth novel. Writing it and finally bringing it to completion turned into a major struggle—a battle with himself over the meaning of what he was doing; a wrestling match with discipline in a not-yet-structured situation; and a dealing with the sheer difficulty of finding words to express his vision. He felt under pressure to produce something to validate his sense of calling. There were also the nagging questions that plague most authors in midpassage about whether the book was worth writing.

What eventually emerged from this many-sided conflict was *The Entrance to Porlock.* The title, Buechner notes, refers to "the visitor from Porlock who woke Coleridge out of the visionary trance of *Kubla Khan,* and what it was essentially about, I think, was the tension between everyday reality and the reality of dream, of imagination" (*NT,* 81).

During the same period he also found time to bring together two volumes of his sermons from Exeter, *The Magnificent Defeat* and *The Hungering Dark.* He was winning the struggle to achieve schedule and discipline.

It was by no means clear, however, that he had won the battle for a sense of meaning in his ministry. Despite successfully completing the novel and pulling together the sermons, Buechner remained dissatisfied. He had the feeling that he had written himself into a dead end.

> There was no farther I could go in that direction. And I felt that in a sense I had lived myself into a blank wall too. I was a minister without a church, a teacher without students, a writer without a subject. I looked to my wife and daughters for more than any human being can give to another. I felt like a rat in a trap, and the trap I was in was myself and the new life I had chosen. (*NT,* 82)

Buechner was trying to find his ministry as a writer. The development that had taken place as he taught and preached in the boys school had brought him to a maturity of perspective that cried out for expression. But he had not found the voice that would be adequate in carrying out his ministry as novelist/theologian, as storyteller/preacher, as artist/evangelist. What was required appeared to be nothing less than another "conversion." The lost had to be found once again.

This second crisis of his life hit while he was trying to complete *The Entrance to Porlock*. From reading it I find it scarcely possible to comprehend Buechner's statement that the labor of writing that book "was so painful that I find it hard, even now, to see beyond my memory of the pain to whatever merit it may have" (*NT,* 81). Through the turmoil of this dark time when he felt caught in a cul-de-sac of his own making, Buechner discovered that the way out was nothing less than the way back into himself. It was a revolutionary insight for him. What it meant was that his best source of material upon which to build his writing was his own experience. For a shy, reticent, buttoned-down easterner, trained by family and his Ivy League education to conceal himself, nothing could have been more difficult than deciding to expose his own thoughts and experiences. As he wrestled with the preparation of some lectures, he made the breakthrough that enabled him to make such a decision.

Charles Price, chaplain at Harvard, had written asking Buechner to deliver the Noble Lectures. When Buechner wrote back, wondering what he might lecture about, Price suggested that he could talk about "religion and letters." The word *letters* struck a responsive chord in Buechner and led him to produce the lectures published as *The Alphabet of Grace*. He chose to explore his own daily round of activities and what of God could be found in the ordinary experiences of his life. When he tried this approach, it became much like Jacob's wrestling with the angel. He persevered and, like Jacob, received a blessing: he discovered a way out of the trap in which he had found himself. As he became willing to expose his own life to his hearers and readers, what had seemed a dead end street turned into a thoroughfare. "What I started trying to do as a writer and as a preacher," he writes, "was more and more to draw on my own experience not just as a source of plot, character, illustration, but as a source of truth" (*NT,* 87). He had found his ministry at last, and he knew it.

LIBERATION: THE GOSPEL ACCORDING TO LEO BEBB

After the agony of completing *Entrance to Porlock,* this insight that came through writing the Noble Lectures provided real catharsis for Buechner. It prepared him for the experience that opened the way to an unanticipated fulfillment of his ministry—the fateful meeting with Leo Bebb.

Around the time that he was preparing to give the Noble Lectures, Buechner's imagination introduced him to this surprising character, one destined to give a new turn and zest to his writing. He recalls it this way:

> I was reading a magazine as I waited my turn at a barber shop one day when, triggered by a particular article and the photograph that went with it, there floated up out of some hitherto unexplored subcellar of me a character who was to dominate my life as a writer for the next six years and more. He was a plump, bald, ebullient southerner who had once served five years in a prison on a charge of exposing himself before a group of children and was now the head of a religious diploma mill in Florida and of a seedy, flat-roofed stucco church called the Church of Holy Love, Incorporated. He wore a hat that looked too small for him. He had a trick eyelid that every once in a while fluttered shut on him. His name was Leo Bebb. (*NT*, 97)

Bebb not only emerged from wherever literary characters come from to dominate Buechner's work. Buechner also acknowledges, correctly, I am convinced, that he found in the character of Leo Bebb a freedom for his writing and for himself that he had never known before.

The liberation that began with *The Alphabet of Grace* and was carried forward by Leo Bebb involved another change. Buechner shifted from the impersonal third-person narrator to the first person. In doing this he found the voice and perspective appropriate for the covenantal union of fiction and faith. To an interviewer who asked him about his use of the first-person narrator, Buechner responded:

> It seems to me to loosen up the whole process of writing. You sound like a person talking instead of like some Olympian deity who sits on high and knows everything. And it allows you, as in conversation, to be quirkish, to take side trips, to stick not quite so relentlessly to what the book is "about." It is also closer to what I seem to be doing more and more in my writing: that is, telling my own tale. Using a first-person narrator allows me to tell a tale as if

it *were* mine. And that puts it just one step, instead of maybe three steps, away from reality.[19]

After discovering Bebb, Buechner originally projected only one novel about this ex-con who ordained people to ministry by mail. But in the process of writing *Lion Country,* something happened to Buechner much like what happened to his narrator in the book, Antonio Parr, in his encounter with Bebb: he became involved and couldn't let go. Buechner found that he could not stop with only one novel about Bebb and the other characters around him, and further, he discovered that writing about them became easier and easier.

The words flowed more quickly as new ideas, people, and situations tumbled over one another in Buechner's imagination. Not only were the words easier, the language he was using suddenly became saltier and funnier than in his previous fiction. He discovered new dimensions within himself, a deeper aliveness that Bebb seemed to evoke in him. "It was from Bebb," he confesses, "that I learned to be braver about exposing myself and my own story" (*NT,* 101). For a self-contained Princeton-educated easterner, this was indeed a tremendous accomplishment. And what was more important, Buechner loved it.

The result of this invasion by Bebb and the rich array of characters he brought with him was the series of four novels: *Lion Country* (1971), *Open Heart* (1972), *Love Feast* (1974), and *Treasure Hunt* (1977). All of them are, as we saw earlier, a marvelous combination of unforgettable characters, fascinating events, and penetrating humor. And, crucial to this book, these novels exemplify in a special way Buechner's unique combination of art and theology.

Bebb and the novels about him acted as inspiration and catalyst for Buechner. The freedom he found there infected his nonfiction. In *Wishful Thinking: A Theological ABC,* for example, Buechner sought to define some of "the great religious words . . . not in any definitive or heavily theological way but in as fresh a way as I could find for restoring to them some of their original life and depth and power" (*NT,* 95). When we read the results of this attempt, we recognize the Bebbsian whimsy that has grasped Buechner and enabled him to revivify with angular insight and delightful humor notions that had become far too heavy to convey their "heavenly" meaning. We see that same liberation of imagination in *Peculiar Treasures,* a book about which Buechner says, "I tried to do the same thing with a hundred or so characters out of the Bible, beginning with Aaron and ending with Zaccheus —tried to scrape off some of the veneer with which centuries of reverence had encrusted them until I reached something at least approaching, I hoped, what had once been their flesh-and-blood humanity" (*NT,* 95–96).

The same freedom informs *Telling the Truth: The Gospel as Tragedy, Comedy, and Fairy Tale,* his Lyman Beecher Lectures at Yale. The subject is preachers and preaching. Buechner begins with a distinctly Bebbsian view of Henry Ward Beecher in New Haven in 1872 ready to deliver the first series of Beecher Lectures, recently established in memory of his father. The younger Beecher is about to be exposed back in his home church in Brooklyn as guilty of adultery. Buechner suggests that preaching involves some self-exposure because preachers as well as their parishioners are people of flesh and blood, human, or at least on their way to being human (*TT,* 3).

The next novel Buechner wrote after completing the Bebb tetralogy was *Godric,* the story of the unlikely, reluctant saint from the Middle Ages. A great sinner for the first part of his life, Godric turns to prayer and hermitry for the next sixty years. Yet, as with Bebb, charlatanry and holiness persistently play hide and seek in Godric's action and influence.

Out of his experiences and adventures in the worlds of Bebb and Godric, Buechner acquired the courage to write two volumes of his autobiography—*The Sacred Journey* and *Now and Then.* The same air of freedom about his own experience that emerged when he met Bebb permeates these books when the subject is explicitly himself. Although his self-exposure does not take him as far as Bebb went, both volumes are impressively personal in ways that would have been impossible for him in the 1950s or 1960s.

Buechner keeps on growing. *Godric* especially illustrates how he continues to develop as both artist and theologian. He apparently started out with the intention of making Godric an earlier incarnation of Leo Bebb, suggested perhaps by the belief in reincarnation held by Gertrude Conover, a Theosophist friend of Bebb's. But the medieval setting of *Godric* involves a totally different landscape from that found in the Bebb novels. And further, though a similarity remains between Bebb and Godric, the character of the uncertain saint changed as Buechner became involved with him. Instead of being an earlier version of Bebb, Godric took on new dimensions and compelled Buechner to grow. He became for Buechner a metaphor for growing old and facing the approach of one's own death. Godric presents a pattern for aging and dying that makes them acceptable, even creative. As happened with Bebb, Godric drew Buechner into a world of deeper experience than he had thought possible.

Since *Godric,* Buechner has published a new novel, *Brendan,* this time about a sixth-century saint. As with his earlier work, it wells up from Buechner's questing faith and impels him toward further spiritual growth. Buechner's novels, like those of Anthony Trollope, are not only stories but also the channel for his ministry. Through the entire range of his artistic production, Buechner has discovered a way that makes it possible for him to carry out his vocation as novelist/theologian.

CHAPTER 5

Distinctive Themes and Perspectives

In *Four Quartets* T. S. Eliot speaks of repeating "Something I have said before. I shall say it again" ("East Coker," 1.134). So let me repeat. We could view Buechner only as a novelist and find in him more than enough to satisfy our longing for interesting stories, well told. It is possible also, though somewhat more difficult, to see him only as a theologian, at work in imaginative ways to proclaim Christian faith so as to evoke deep and lasting response. As I have read and reread Buechner's books, I have been caught by a particular atmosphere that he creates in all his writing. He draws me into a context with a living wholeness that will not let me call him *either* novelist *or* theologian. He is both at once.

He achieves this living wholeness through his skill as a superb storyteller. His characters, images, scenes, and turns of phrase and thought are comparable to the best that the literature of the English language offers. And there is more. As we come to dwell fully in the world he weaves around us, theological questions are inescapably present within the enveloping action of his narrative and enter our awareness with pervasive insistence.

As I saw that Buechner must be viewed as novelist/theologian, not as one or the other, the integration of events and themes into the probing perspective of religious faith emerged for me with clarity. The artistic scope of faith and the religious depth in Buechner appeared to me with the suddenness of a thunderclap of silence.

Why should this seem unusual? The Bible is filled with well-told yarns. It includes story, biography, history, and poetic narrative that embody the believed-in realities and deepest faith of the Hebrew and Christian communities. The same integration of faith and art can be found elsewhere, for example, in Homer and in the *Iliad*, as well as in the great literature of other traditions. It is also true that many great writers, like many good artists, give careful attention to the inclusive, theological dimensions of their work. What struck me suddenly was the company in which Buechner belonged—Dante, Milton, Dostoevsky.

Among twentieth-century novelists whose writing illustrates a careful integration of theological elements into their stories, I think first of Alan Paton in *Cry, the Beloved Country*. The sins of humanity are closely interwoven with the grace of God in the social patterns of South Africa as Paton depicts them in his powerful novel. Human acts of injustice, murder, and retribution are related inseparably to God's action of bringing righteousness, redemption, and love into the patterns of human interaction. Paton makes it clear that tragedy and forgiveness in the contemporary world call us to faith as surely as any biblical parable or evangelist's preaching. James Gould Cozzens's novels have their carefully crafted theological themes. In *By Love Possessed,* the climactic moment of illumination occurs in a garden with a man, a woman, and a snake. Others might recall Andrew Lytle's *Velvet Horn*, a novel built around a mystery, the solution of which involves a fascinating reworking of the biblical story of creation. As theologian, Buechner brings the encompassing perspective and the depth of probing into the human situation that is essential to every superb novelist.

Artists of genuine stature have never found the dimensions of faith foreign to their work. It needs to be noted also that theologians are emerging from the arid wastelands of pedantic rationalism and rediscovering the artistic character of religious expression. As this book's coauthor puts it, we are recovering "the impulse toward saga, story, and parable prominent in all religious traditions and especially significant in the Hebrew and Christian Scriptures."[20] H. Richard Niebuhr also affirms the historical, story-filled form of theology as essential to the Christian community. He writes:

> Yet what prompted Christians in the past to confess their faith by telling the story of their life was more than a need for vivid illustration or for analogical reasoning. . . . Their story was not a parable which could be replaced by another; it was irreplaceable and untranslatable. . . . We find that we must travel the road which has been taken by our predecessors in the Christian community. . . . Whether this be true of other faiths than Christianity, we may not be sure, but it seems very true of our faith.[21]

As novelist/theologian, then, Buechner is doing nothing less than what every great writer must do and striving for nothing more than others who seek to set forth biblical Christian faith with human wholeness.

In this chapter I shall attempt to articulate the special ambience that Buechner creates through the use of distinctive themes and perspectives. Their implications for theological reflection will become obvious, I think, as we move through them, and the way he incarnates them in his storytelling provides us with a sense of their connection with our own experience.

Each of the themes I present has its own specific meaning and can be delineated separately from the others. When viewed together in their interrelationship, they constitute a sketch of the Christian theology embodied in Buechner's work as novelist, storyteller, and preacher.

THE SACREDNESS OF ORDINARY HUMAN EXPERIENCE

Joseph Conrad writes that, given all that binds humanity together, "there is not a place of splendour or a dark corner of the earth that does not deserve attention, if only a passing glance of wonder and pity." Buechner's sense of that covenantal bonding is even stronger than Conrad's in that he sees the binding together taking place in God.

Nothing is clearer in Buechner's writings than the notion that God is present throughout the entirety of human experience. There is no sector that is secular; every part is sacred and may become in any moment and in unexpected ways a window through which we see God or a hand with which the divine reaches out to grasp us. It is always a matter of listening to our lives with the sensitivity that can perceive God's presence with us.

In one of his sermons, Buechner says:

> We all want to be certain, we all want proof, but the kind of proof that we tend to want — scientifically or philosophically demonstrable proof that would silence all doubts once and for all — would not in the long run, I think, answer the fearful depths of our need at all. For what we need to know, of course, is not just that God exists, not just that beyond the steely brightness of the stars there is a cosmic intelligence of some kind that keeps the whole show going, but that there is a God right here in the thick of our day-to-day lives who may not be writing messages about deity in

the stars but who in one way or another is trying to get messages through our blindness as we move around down here knee-deep in the fragrant muck and misery and marvel of the world. It is not objective proof of God's existence that we want but, whether we use religious language for it or not, the experience of God's presence. That is the miracle that we are really after. And that is also, I think, the miracle that we really get. (*MD*, 47)

Although the sacredness of ordinary experience is affirmed, Buechner does not suggest that God can be seen easily or in obvious form anywhere. There is a hiddenness about deity, but not a hiddenness that is revealed only in particular sacred locations or by a particular sacred priesthood. God's presence is in all experience, often in places where we least anticipate it. God speaks through experiences that seem strange to the ecclesiastically orthodox, and is available to all humans, however twisted and alienated they may appear to our normal ways of viewing. What is required in order to perceive the divine is deepened awareness, listening. "Be still and know that I am God" (Ps. 46:10) is a theme that pervades Buechner's writing.

In an article that I have found both interesting and helpful, Rudolph L. Nelson suggests that "the mystical experience has been a continuing theme in Buechner's novels."[22] Beginning with Buechner's saying, "Mysticism is where religions start" (*WT*, 64), Nelson traces this theme through some of the novels. In *The Seasons' Difference*, for example, Peter Cowley's mystical vision disturbs the peace of some vacationing families, who would prefer not to be bothered. The book ends indecisively as to whether Peter's vision is accepted as real, but, as Nelson puts it, he "has succeeded in forcing the group to confront the possibility and threat of transcendence."[23] In *The Final Beast*, as Nelson sees it, Buechner goes much further and is clearly "incarnating in fictional form the stage of the mystic way which [Evelyn] Underhill identifies as the illumination of the self."[24] Peter Ringkoping in *The Entrance to Porlock* has experiences of mystical illumination. In the "tetralogy of novels about evangelist Leo Bebb," says Nelson, ". . . Buechner is back at his old stand . . ." and "religious concerns are paramount." Contrasting the Bebb novels with *The Final Beast* and *Porlock*, Nelson continues:

When the theme of mystical illumination makes its way into

this fictional world [of Bebb], it is not the straightforward religious imagery of *The Final Beast* (nothing is played straight in the world of Leo Bebb) or in the secular idiom of *Porlock* (all of the irony and Rabelaisian humor notwithstanding, Antonio is finally on a genuine search for some kind of valid religious truth). What Buechner does, on two occasions, is to *re*mythologize the theme of mystical illumination.[25]

This theme occurs the first time when Bebb tells his wife, Lucille, of Herman Redpath's trip to the happy-hunting ground. The second time it occurs is when Antonio shares some of John Turtle's "Puff-Puff." "Call it dream, call it hallucinogenic trip, it is also mystical illumination. For Antonio it is finally a healing vision."[26]

Nelson directs our attention to a crucial aspect of Buechner's novels. It seems necessary to me, however, to change the focus slightly in order to understand exactly what Buechner means as well as to make clear the dimensions of his artistic achievement. The mystical and transcendent often are taken in the Western religious tradition to mean the experience of something outside of and beyond our ordinary perception that illumines the everyday realm of living. Encounter with the extraordinary provides the insight that illumines the ordinary. This seems to be the view that Nelson has and thinks that Buechner shares.

There is also present in our tradition a somewhat different understanding of the mystical and the transcendent. In this other view, human experience never goes beyond the ordinary in a way that provides a clear view of God and eternity in the light of which the ordinary can be seen for what it really is. We remain immersed in the ordinary, but certain "ordinary" occurrences grasp us, make us listen, and become a key by means of which we believe we can understand the whole of our experience. Some particular part of the ordinary becomes extraordinary by serving as a light, sometimes dim and flickering, by which the rest of the ordinary takes on meaning. The mystical in life happens, as we seek and strain for some meaning in it all, when we discover something in the usual round taking hold of us. We may even believe that God has spoken to us. In the same way, the transcendent is not beyond and apart from the ordinary but some part of experience leaps out at us, calls forth faith within us at least for a moment, and, transcending other parts in significance, becomes the means for seeing some wholeness in the tangle of events making up our life.

This latter view, I believe, fits with what Buechner would have learned from Tillich, Muilenburg, or Reinhold Niebuhr, and what he would have discovered from reading H. Richard Niebuhr. It is, I believe, what we find in his writing and, as we shall see, it provides a central way for understanding his fusion of theology and art, faith and fiction.

For me, one of the best illustrations of his conviction that the sacred permeates the entirety of ordinary human experience occurs in *The Final Beast*. It is the passage I have already quoted in Chapter 2 that deals with Nicolet's experience of the clack-clack of branches as he is still and listening and waiting for God. In the midst of the mundane, we can expect God and may perhaps encounter God.

I have used this example from Buechner in worship services and in classes. When I do, I always bring two branches along and, when reading the passage from the novel that sets the distinctive context, I hit the limbs together so that those present can actually hear with Nicolet "the approach of the approach perhaps of splendor" and be prepared to listen with Buechner to their lives with expanding awareness. The simple act of striking the branches together suggests the potential for the mystical within the mundane—for those ready to perceive it.

REDEMPTION AND GRACE IN THE WHOLE CREATION, INCLUDING THE RIDICULOUS AND THE OBSCENE

As God is present to us throughout the range of ordinary experience, so God redeems not just part, but the entirety, of creation. As Buechner sees it, this means redemption of everything, especially those sectors we may think beyond the possibility of redemption or even unworthy of redemption. The humorous and the ridiculous are for certain, in Buechner's view, parts of the creation that are being redeemed. And also the obscene.

"Though we make our bed in hell, thou art there," says the psalmist. Not only is God there, but, in Jesus Christ on the cross, God takes on the pain and tragedy that are the hells and final obscenities of this world. To make it even clearer, Buechner in *The Final Beast* depicts God as taking on the shit of this world. But, of course, what the image of excrement becomes as Buechner expands it into symbol is sin. God in Jesus Christ takes on the worst the world has to offer, the worst we can give, and still redeems it.

The other side of the matter needs to be remembered also. If the whole creation, including the ridiculous and the obscene, is being redeemed, then it is equally true that anything in creation can be used by God in the process of redeeming the whole. This insight may come as a shock to people accustomed to the moralism of ordinary parish existence in our churches.

I remember a woman who took a class called Theology and Literature that my husband, Charles, and I taught for students in training to be ministers at Pacific School of Religion and the Graduate Theological Union. This particular student was somewhat older than the average seminarian, a member of that increasing group of people who decide in their thirties or forties, rather than in their twenties just after finishing college, to attend seminary and seek ordination in one or another denomination.

Among the varied authors whose work we read and discussed in the class was Frederick Buechner. And, of course, we read the novels about Leo Bebb. This student, whom we shall here call Pat (to protect the guilty, I suppose, as well as the innocent), was visibly shocked by the characters, their behavior, and especially the language used. In class we read some of the material aloud, with each person sharing in the reading. Pat first tried to read, stammered over some of the obscenities, and then said she could not say such filthy words out loud in a group. Later she came to us and said that she did not believe words like those Buechner used (*shit* somehow seemed worst of all to her) could have any place in the speech of Christians. Furthermore, she could not understand what possible place such language and such literature could have in the curriculum of a theological seminary. Perhaps, she concluded, she ought to drop the class.

We asked her if she had heard obscenities used as she was growing up. Yes, she said, but not in church. Did she think, we queried, that not talking about it made it any less real or present in the "nonchurch" lives of people? No, she admitted. Did she believe that God was redeeming the entire world, and that this somehow had to include what the polite society of our upbringing ignored, repressed, or tried to name in euphemistic ways in an attempt to dodge the seamier side of human existence?

After thinking about these questions, still with some doubts remaining, she decided to continue in the course. She learned to say the forbidden words and, even better, to see what Buechner was doing by using them. Two years later, when she was ready to graduate and be ordained, she came to me and thanked me for the class. What she went through in coming to terms with Buechner's outrageous characters and obscene language had been, she said, the most significant learning experience of her preparation for ministry. Without it, she would have been unable to face the less respectable, and crucially important, sectors of human experience that Jesus came especially to redeem. Reading Buechner had become a landmark experience for this person.

Grace, for Buechner, comes when it is least expected, often in situations of ambiguity and contradiction or through people whose intentions are not particularly good, nor are their motives pure. Is Leo Bebb, for example, a charlatan or a saint? Or is he both? Or does it matter whether he is either, both, or neither if what he gives to people is a life that burns a little hotter and shines a little brighter?

Rain falls on the just and the unjust, and grace appears from sources that cannot be distinguished on moral grounds. God's grace and redemption are present throughout the whole of creation, including, especially, the ridiculous and the obscene. Ordinary experience is not only sacred; it is filled with grace. Any person or anything, however unlikely it may appear, can become for us grace-ful.

The invisible manifests itself in the visible. I think of the alphabet, of letters literally—A, B, C, D, E, F, G, all twenty-six of them. I think how poetry, history, the wisdom of the sages and the holiness of the saints, all of this invisible comes down to us dressed out in their visible, alphabetic drab. H and I and J, and K, L, M, N are the mold that our innermost thoughts must be pressed into finally if we are to share them; O, P, Q, R, S, T, U is the wooden tongue that we must speak if we are ever to make ourselves known, that must be spoken to us if we are ever to know. V, W, X, Y, Z. Clack-clack. . . .

I am thinking of grace. I am thinking of power beyond all power, the power that holds all things in manifestation, and I am thinking of this power as ultimately a Christ-making power, which is to say a power that makes Christs, which is to say a power that works through the drab and hubbub of our lives to make Christs of us before we're done or else, for our sakes, graciously to destroy us. In neither case, needless to say, is the process to be thought of as painless. (*AG*, 10–11)

THE SEARCH TO BE KNOWN, TO BE FORGIVEN, TO BE HEALED, TO BE LOVED

In *The Alphabet of Grace* (55–57), Buechner tells of a time when he and his wife joined a group-dynamics group that met, as he puts it delicately, "for what was only a month or two but seemed a whole long and painful adolescence." On one occasion, with the honesty those groups encourage and sometimes do indeed produce, Buechner blurted out his annoyance with another member who had taken attention away from him. A teaching colleague in the group said, "That's all right, Freddy. Don't be upset. We love you too." For Buechner, those words became a miracle from a most unlikely source. He reflects on the incident:

> Whatever "we love you" means, he meant—that at least for a moment they had seen who I was, really was more or less who it was who had been sitting there in that face all those weeks awaiting and dreading his time, and they wished me well, they willed my good, my peace. It was only then that I realized that this was why I had kept coming all those weeks and why perhaps they had all of them kept coming, perhaps even in some sense why I have come here to speak to you now and why you have come to listen: to be known, to be forgiven, to be healed, which I suppose is to say, if the word is not beyond all hope of salvage, to be loved. This ancient and most holy miracle. (*AG*, 57)

These words seem to me to sum up the hope and the quest of his characters, of Buechner himself in his life and in his writing, and indeed of most of us on our individual sacred journeys.

THE PRESENCE OF MEANING IN THE APPARENTLY RANDOM EVENTS OF LIFE

Listen to the sounds of your life, Buechner keeps telling us in a variety of artistic ways. "The crow of a rooster. Two carpenters talking at their work in another room. The tick-tock of a clock on the wall. The rumble of your own stomach. Each sound can be thought of as meaning something, if it is meaning you want" (*SJ*, 76). The meaning that can be meaning for us must come from our own lives and our own experience. And we also have to want to find it there.

It is an all too common thing for us to seek meaning in the lives and experience of others and even to live vicariously through that second-hand meaning. Buechner sees how stories from other places and other lives can illumine our own experience. Perhaps, he suggests, it is not the task of theology and art to amuse us with alien meanings and other worlds, but instead to help us find our own meaning in our own world. They do so by helping us discover that God is incarnate in our own lives, in our particular locations, on our sacred journeys.

He writes:

> The question is not whether the things that happen to you are chance things or God's things because, of course, they are both at once. There is no chance thing through which God cannot speak— even the walk from the house to the garage that you have walked ten thousand times before, even the moments when you cannot believe there is a God who speaks at all anywhere. God speaks, I believe, and the words are incarnate in the flesh and blood of our selves and of our own footsore and sacred journeys. (*SJ*, 77)

The results of this insight seem to be embodied in Buechner's own experience. As he is working on the plots for his novels, he comes to realize and discover that his own life has a plot too. In the process, as he draws us into his stories, we may begin listening to our own experiences and come alive to the meaning present there, in what may have appeared before as random, meaningless happenings.

> God speaks to us through our lives, we often too easily say. *Something* speaks anyway, spells out some sort of godly or godforsaken meaning to us through the alphabet of our years, but often it takes many years and many further spellings out before we start to glimpse, or think we do, a little of what that meaning is. Even then we glimpse it only dimly, like the first trace of dawn on the rim of night, and even then it is a meaning that we cannot fix and be sure of once and for all because it is always incarnate meaning and thus as alive and changing as we are ourselves alive and changing. (*SJ*, 41)

THE BLESSEDNESS OF COMEDY, LAUGHTER, AND THE ANTIC STYLE

At the very beginning, in the introduction, I said that Buechner's artistry takes place among confession, and tears, and great laughter. He has a gift for perceiving all three together in any situation, and then showing God present with us in all of them. James Muilenburg, Buechner's Old Testament professor at Union Seminary, lived out the combination in his teaching. Nicolet, the minister in *The Final Beast,* for all his sorrow and falteringly firm faith, is a comic, clownish figure.

Nowhere in his writing does the antic emerge more clearly than in the Bebb novels. Leo Bebb himself, with his trick eyelid and his often tricky life, provides the best illustrations of the laughter at the core of Buechner's vision. But there is no stranger example than the Joking Cousin of Herman Redpath's Indian family. Antonio Parr goes to Texas to attend the ceremonies surrounding Herman Redpath's death. His curiosity is aroused by what seems to him the eccentric behavior of many mourners, especially one of them.

> After the funeral was over, Bebb was able to explain to me at least something about the eccentric behavior of John Turtle, but at the time I was unprepared for it. Bebb said, "Seems like every one of your big family groups has got what they call a Joking Cousin, and for Herman Redpath's family group it's John Turtle. A Joking Cousin's main job is to make jokes, but he doesn't make your run-of-the-mill jokes, and he doesn't make them at run-of-the-mill times either. Say there's a marriage being arranged and the heads of both families are there all dressed up to make terms. Or say a man's dying or just died and the women have come over to pay their last respects. Maybe a girl gets herself in trouble, and there's a pow-wow what to do about finding her a husband. They're the times when the Joking Cousin does his stuff. Seems as if the Joking Cousin is the Indians themselves mocking and blaspheming their own holiest times so as nobody else will. Seems to me like an Indian thinks if he mocks the holiest times he's got, maybe then the evil spirits will be fooled into letting the holy times alone. Maybe even God will let them alone then, Antonio." (*OH* in *BB,* 150).

Though uncertain just how much Bebb's explanation explained, Antonio reports some peculiar examples of the behavior of John Turtle as the Joking Cousin during Herman Redpath's funeral in the Church of Holy Love. Bebb was leading the service.

> "I am the resurrection and the life," Bebb said from the pulpit pale as death, and John Turtle stood behind him holding two fingers up over Bebb's head like rabbit ears. . . .
>
> "The Lord is my shepherd, I shall not want," Bebb read from the lectern, his face glistening with perspiration, and "I know what *you* want right enough," John Turtle said from the foot of the casket.
>
> Bebb said, "He maketh me to lie down in green pastures, He leadeth me beside the still waters," and John Turtle said, "I know a girl what lives on a hill. If she won't do it, her sister will." You have to hand it to Bebb. He never batted an eye. (*OH* in *BB*, 150)

In *Telling the Truth: The Gospel as Tragedy, Comedy, and Fairy Tale*, Buechner talks about the "comedy of God's saving the most unlikely people when they least expect it, the joke in which God laughs with humanity and humanity with God" (*TT*, 72). The comic is no less at the heart of the Gospel than is the tragic, though the long faces in church have forgotten how to laugh. When Jesus told stories they were antic, comic, filled with jokes:

> I mean the kind of joke Jesus told when he said it is harder for a rich person to enter Paradise than for a Mercedes to get through a revolving door, harder for a rich person to enter Paradise than for Nelson Rockefeller to get through the night deposit slot of the First National City Bank. And then added that though for humans it is impossible, for God all things are possible because God is the master of the impossible. . . . It seems to me that more often than not the parables can be read as high and holy jokes about God and about humanity and about the Gospel itself as the highest and holiest joke of them all. (*TT*, 63)

The comic style Buechner prizes is not found in a derisive kind of laughter that scorns or makes fun of something or belittles people in the midst of their difficulties. Rather it is a sense that within and beyond the hard times there is a presence that wishes us well and will sustain us.

THE PRECARIOUS NATURE OF LIFE AND RELATIONSHIPS ENHANCES MEANING EXPERIENCED IN THE PRESENT

Buechner has a profound sense of the chancy and contingent character of life as we experience it. Things can go in any one of a variety of alternative ways, depending on seemingly insignificant occurrences. "On such slender chances hang the destinies of us all," Antonio Parr says about a remark by Gertrude Conover that galvanized Leo Bebb into action (*LF* in *BB*, 298). Phrases similar to this one appear often in Buechner's writing. In this way he underscores and reminds us of the incidental, seemingly accidental, presence of grace in our lives and in history.

Undoubtedly, Buechner brings this perception from his own life. Many experiences, especially the suicides of his father and later of his uncle, must have produced and enhanced this awareness. He says that in some ways this makes him a worrier, because he often expects the worst. But, quite clearly, it has also endowed him with a fuller sense of the present moment and the importance of living deeply in every *now*.

FAITH AS THE BELIEF THAT THE WORST THING IS NEVER THE LAST THING

In this attempt to summarize Buechner's "credo" there is a conclusion that permeates and informs all else. In the midst of his commitment to God and the varied expressions of this commitment, there is this *Te Deum*. When we are experiencing terrible things, we know that the worst thing is only the next to the last thing that will happen. And we know this by faith.

Of the time at Phillips Exeter, after the publication of *The Return of Ansel Gibbs*, Buechner writes:

> I was too occupied with my job to think much about the next novel I myself might write, but it occurred to me that, if and when the time ever came, it would be the presence of God rather than God's absence that I would write about, of death and dark and despair as not the last reality but only the next to the last. (*NT*, 49)

The Final Beast can be seen as a parable embodying this theme, but the message runs deeply throughout all of Buechner's subsequent work. Perhaps he is trying to capture in artistic form what Paul Tillich says of Martin Luther:

> Luther had experiences which he describes as attacks of utter despair (*Anfechtung*), as the frightful threat of a complete meaninglessness. He felt these moments as satanic attacks in which everything was menaced: his Christian faith, the confidence in his work, the Reformation, the forgiveness of sins. Everything broke down in the extreme moments of this despair, nothing was left of the courage to be. Luther in these moments, and in the descriptions he gives of them, anticipated the descriptions of them by modern Existentialism. But for him this was not the last word. The last word was the first commandment, the statement that God is God. It reminded him of the unconditional element in human experience of which one can be aware even in the abyss of meaninglessness. And this awareness saved him.[27]

In *The Final Beast*, when Rooney Vail has disappeared, giving her husband, Clem, no notice or reason, as she had done once before in the midst of their honeymoon in Austria, Theodore Nicolet, her pastor, sets out to find her. She may need help, or he may be able to persuade her to return.

On the bus heading for Muscadine, he carries on a silent conversation with Franny, his dead wife, or with Christ, or with Harold, his daughter Cornelia's name for God—"Our Father who aren't in heaven," she prays in her five-year-old way, "Harold be thy name" (*FB*, 33). And at the end of the bus line, he starts hitchhiking to Muscadine. Then comes a passage that says what faith is all about probably as well as humans can say it.

> Leaving behind him his children, his church, and begging a ride to a town that he had never heard of to find a young woman who had written that she would be thinking of him in Muscadine, but not to follow her there—he wondered. . . . He was not really sure why he was going to Muscadine or why Rooney herself had gone.
> But instead of disturbing him, this made him feel suddenly stupid and gay. . . . It was good to be going and not to know why; if

you waited until you knew why, you would never go anywhere. It was faith, after all: simply to go—to have as having not, to grasp nothing but always to hold in the open palm of your hand. (*FB*, 44–45)

As has become clear in the discussion of each of them, the themes I have mentioned are closely interrelated. It has also become plain that the themes are distinctive in Buechner's work because they show the novelist and theologian as inseparable and demonstrate the unity of fiction and faith as integral to his writing. Perhaps it will be helpful to review the themes and make explicit the symbiotic relation between art and faith.

1. Ordinary human experience can appear to have a miscellaneous quality. It may have a certain coherence but not an obvious, clear meaning. If we listen to our experience and are really seeking meaning, then the ordinary will yield up a depth of significance we had not thought was there. For Christian faith, this means that *in and through* our everyday experience a sacredness is present to us that can provide *illumination* for our life's journey.

2. Social convention gives greater honor to certain positions and particular ways of speaking and acting. Experience as it comes to us teaches us to regard parts of it as good and desirable and other parts as ridiculous and obscene. But all areas of life together, whether regarded as high or low, make up the whole of the world. All parts are there and must be fitted into whatever meaning we find. In Christian faith we speak then of the *up and down* of the world and the *reconciliation* and redemption of it all, even the ridiculous and the obscene.

3. For Buechner, however, there is more meaning to be found in our lives than even illumination and redemption. In the depth of the mystery, there is grace. Ambiguity characterizes all the circumstances of human experience. In the ambiguity there is often also the sense of paradox and contradiction. The mystery often appears to be a void, a bottomless abyss of possibility. And in the midst of tragedy, Mystery takes on the appearance of Enemy that destroys all that which we love and all that to which we give our loyalty. But as we listen to our lives, the mystery can resolve itself into grace. *Now and then* the grace of God shines through the ambiguity and contradiction and becomes for us the *incarnation* of the divine, the light that the darkness does not overcome, the presence of God with us.

4. All of us are on the way, on the journey that constitutes our living. This journey is not just a trip. It is a quest, a search to be known, to be forgiven, to be healed, and to be loved. As light illumines our path and reconciliation takes place, we have glimpses of meaning on our way. What turns the trip into a sacred journey is discovering that our search is overtaken by One who seeks us. When the mystery becomes grace, the experience is less one of finding meaning than of encountering the Source of meaning. As H. Richard Niebuhr put it, "We sought a good to love and were found by a good that loves us." So *once and for all*, the lost is found and our search is being satisfied yet also nullified by the *revelation* of the very selfhood of God.

5. Then the way in which the apparently random events of life take on pattern and meaning no longer seems strange. What happens to us may seems to be exactly what happened before, but it has been changed completely. The mystery that seemed now ambiguous and then contradictory is seen in a new perspective. The now and then of incarnation takes center stage and provides the story that encompasses all that happens to us. The *this and that* of our experience undergoes *transformation* so that the One who met us as the face of the mystery was revealed provides the meaning that includes every event.

6. Yet we find ourselves always on the edge of meaninglessness. We teeter on the brink of nonsense. Only the grace of being able to dissolve tears into laughter staves off the absurd and the tragic. Buechner understands well and shows us vividly the blessedness of comedy and the antic style. As our way is transformed from that of losers traveling in lostness to a sacred journey of the foundering who have been found, our path does not suddenly become straight and plain. Rather it is more *round and about*, amid tears and great laughter, through the comic and the antic dressed up as fantasy and fairy tale, that our lives are caught up in the *transfiguration* that enables us to journey in faith.

7. Our traveling therefore does not take on the security of a Sunday afternoon ride with seat belts carefully buckled. We are not rendered immune to illness and pain and death. The tragic remains both possible and usually present in one guise or another. Now, however, when we continue on our way, the perilous nature of our existence and the precarious character of all the relationships we prize adds depth of meaning to every present. Our senses are attuned to the beauty of this day when we know that our weeks and years are limited. We are able to love with greater awareness when we know that those we love may

be taken from us. *Time and again* the limited, precarious nature of our lives provides *stimulation* to a depth of appreciation we might never know if we thought we would live forever.

8. Buechner's insight into Christian faith goes further. When the revelation of God comes through a meeting with Jesus as the incarnation of the divine, then we are not surprised at the precariousness of life. In the perspective provided by Jesus, all that exists, whether in nature or in history, exhibits the shape of a cross. To recognize the tragic dimension of human life is, in Christian perspective, to know that existence is cruciform. And death on this cross of being is the worst thing we know. But it is not the last thing. *Here and there*, through the interstices of tragedy that seem to mark the bars that imprison us, we are enabled in Christian faith to see beyond and know that the last thing for us is *Resurrection*, a life in God in whom from first to last we live and move and have our being.

In our own experience we sense the wholeness of creation that is in travail, moving through the worst and reaching in hope for the last that is the best. There is both *no and yes* to be heard. To believe that there is a *yes* within and beyond the *no* that tragedy and death speak to us requires faith in God's faithfulness. So it is trust in the *covenant* of God the Faithful One that enables Buechner to keep art and theology appropriately *un*separated.

At one point in *The Final Beast*, Nicolet is trying to collect his thoughts for the next Sunday's sermon, but events and people, especially his dead wife, Franny, keep crowding in. At one point, after a few jottings, he "crossed out what he had written and in block letters wrote, 'IS IT TRUE?' Was that, secretly, what they came to find out Sunday after Sunday, just that, yes or no?" (*FB*, 173). That's the question you avoid like death—or perhaps, even more, like life. And then he imagines what he might say in his sermon:

> "Oh the world's a great bordello all right, saith the prophet—down to the last square inch. What's a minister like me even but God's pimp, maybe half in love with the flesh he's peddling but only half? . . . Beloved, don't believe I preach the best without knowing the worst, that's all I mean. I know it, beloved. . . . But the worst thing isn't the last thing about the world. It's the next to the last thing. The last thing is the best. It's the power from on high that comes down into the world, that wells up from the rock-bottom

worst of the world like a hidden spring. Can you believe it? The last, best thing is the laughing deep in the hearts of the saints, sometimes our hearts even. Yes. You are terribly loved and forgiven. Yes. You are healed. All is well." (*FB*, 174–5)

CHAPTER 6

Literature as Metaphor

A poet friend of mine, Rosalie Moore, has a helpful perspective on Buechner. "He is," she says, "a poet who uses prose, taking experience and transmuting it into a greater dimension—that is, greater than the literal physical reality. A kind of transubstantiation is achieved. In this dimension, the religious and the aesthetic become one." This fits well with my own experience of Buechner's writing. I would even go further and say that he is a poet who uses prose like a painter applies color to canvas. So vivid is his style that I find myself looking back in my mind's eye to his novels as though I had seen a movie. Sharon, with her young thief's smile and her hair blown across her face; Brownie's perpetual smile that displays the even rows of china teeth; Lucille drinking Tropicanas, in her rocking chair on the shaded veranda in sun-drenched Amarillo; Indian chief Herman Redpath with his tightly stretched brown leather for skin; Bebb looking like old-time actor Gene Lockhart, with a trick eyelid; Gertrude Conover with her bluish hair on a head turned a little sideways—I *see* them rather than think about them.

How does Buechner achieve this poet/painter effect? Not with mirrors but with metaphors. He is a poet who works like a painter with characters, events, images, and symbols clothed in metaphorical garb.

In Buechner's "new creation," as I call it, he presents Christian faith in stories developed as parables, through art that incarnates meaning with religious depth, and by means of theology expressed in metaphor. Metaphor, however, occupies a more central place than even that use suggests. Metaphor permeates his writing completely.

In the following passage, Buechner is speaking about Dostoevsky. He reveals at the same time, I am convinced, what he does in his own work and how he uses metaphors:

> In a letter to a friend about *The Brothers Karamazov,*

Dostoevsky wrote, "The chief problem dealt with throughout this particular work is the very one which has, my whole life long, tormented my conscious or subconscious being: the question of the existence of God." Clearly the question was not an academic one for Dostoevsky but a question that arose out of what he calls his tormenting experience, and to put that experience into words he did on a far larger scale what Shakespeare, for instance, did when he wrote "How like a winter hath my absence been from thee." My experience of God and of no-God, Dostoevsky says, is like . . . and then the whole complex structure and treasury of *The Brothers Karamazov* comes forth as a single metaphor which enables us to participate in the depths of that experience as no academic disquisition could ever do. (*RCR*, 179–80)

Buechner, in his own novels, is doing something closely parallel to what he sees Dostoevsky doing. First, his stories emerge from the depth of his questing faith, and second, the treasury of characters and the structure of events embody metaphors pointing toward larger patterns of meaning. In this way his novels, like Dostoevsky's, become a single metaphor reflecting Buechner's experience of God. And because of the vivid metaphorical expression both Buechner and Dostoevsky give their own experience, we who read are drawn in, come to dwell in that experience and find that it illumines our own world and may transform it.

It is important, however, to emphasize what this means about his use of metaphor. Though a novel comes out as a single metaphor, it cannot be understood as a simple metaphor. In Buechner's stories, I have discovered, metaphor follows upon metaphor. They interact with one another and fit together in patterns, making more inclusive metaphors until they form the single metaphor embodied in the enveloping action of the entire book. Perhaps this happens in the work of all great writers, but it is especially and vividly the case in Buechner's novels as I have experienced them.

How does this magic of the imagination take place? We find Buechner giving us some clues in the same essay in which he speaks of Dostoevsky. He is commenting on a brief passage by the great prose stylist and preacher of the early seventeenth century John Donne. In this sermon, Buechner says, Donne conveys not merely information, but an entire range of feelings about God. "Of the devices he uses to convey this complex and ultimately unverbalizable feeling, perhaps the most important is metaphor." Donne refers to God as "the general of a great army," as "the inescapable tenant of the Sea, Heaven, Hell," and as "the custodian of a rich treasure house of mercy to which our sense of sin is the key." What is Donne doing? Buechner says

> In all of this Donne is concerned not so much with illumining our understanding as with enchanting us as he himself is enchanted, with transmitting to us something of his own inner sense of the mystery and majesty of God which in the last analysis words cannot name directly any more than to a blind man words can name directly objects of sight. The sun is like the calling of trumpets, the color green is like the smell of rain, we say to the blind man; and to one who cannot see as Donne sees, cannot feel as Donne feels, Donne says God is like this, God is like that, until we begin to connect his metaphors like points on a graph and come out with a richer sense of the reality of Donne's experience of God than could ever be directly named. (*RCR*, 175–6)

This is exactly what Buechner does. Characters and events dressed in the shining raiment of metaphor pour from his imagination. Because his is an imagination inflamed and intoxicated by God, everything points by reiterated indirection toward God. Metaphor relates to metaphor until a more inclusive metaphor appears. As sentences make a paragraph and paragraphs become chapters, so metaphors fit together into a single great arrow pointing toward God. Even the less imaginative among us may catch the meaning.

And so Buechner brings us to a further insight. He writes, "The truth of it seems to be that it is not only that literature contains metaphors but that literature essentially *is* metaphor" (*RCR*, 179). Susanne K. Langer shares Buechner's view; a work of art, she writes, is "a developed metaphor."[28] And it is this understanding that Buechner illustrates with compelling power in all his writing.

When we remember his view of theology as metaphor and confront now his understanding of literature as essentially metaphor, the unity of faith and art in his work takes on even greater significance. As with Dostoevsky, what emerges through metaphor in Buechner's work are his deepest convictions. Art incarnates what he believes in as an encompassing reality, that is, God. And this believed-in reality is articulated with a power that enables others, even impels them, to listen and perhaps discover that same reality calling to them from the depth of their own experience.

I am not suggesting that all art is somehow covertly Christian. Not at all. But I am affirming with Buechner that art emerges from human experience, from human communities of faith and interpretation. Art reflects our experience and conveys our convictions about a reality, or a deity, we believe in as ultimate. The shape of experience, as given through the meaning and faith present in the characters and events in Buechner's novels, becomes the shape of God in the total story as borne in metaphor.

It comes as no surprise, then, that in Buechner's writing we find metaphor tumbling after metaphor like leaves in autumn. No, that is not quite right. To put it better, metaphor fits with metaphor, building one upon another, leaves hanging together until they merge into the large image of a tree. The final impact of a Buechner novel is not, then, metaphors and metaphors whirling around like leaves in the wind, but rather metaphors conveyed in character and event, image and symbol, that are leaves integrated into increasingly inclusive patterns adding up at last to a towering tree of life.

The "leaves" making up the "tree" that is a completed novel for Buechner are characters that act and interact within a plot and fictional landscape, images that put the stamp of meaning on the events the characters are experiencing, and symbols that point beyond the immediate experience to possible meanings that embrace the wholeness of living. Each of these—character, event, image, symbol— becomes dwelt-in and believed-in reality through the power of metaphor.

CHARACTERS AND EVENTS

The Buechner novel that illustrates most clearly, it seems to me, his understanding of literature as essentially metaphor is *The Entrance to Porlock*. The characters, all of them, are saturated with reality. The events as they unfold could almost, but not quite, have happened to me. As the plot develops, however, these people, and what they do, exist in a metaphor-lighted world.

"Room!" Peter Ringkoping says in the opening sentence, as if to tell us that he is interested in space, so much so that he seems "spaced out," if not "spacey." As he watches a band concert on the town common one summer, he sees the trumpet player "letting out great raspberries of sound" with "cheeks puffed out like the North Wind on an old map." And then he sees "a panel of air behind the bandstand swing open like a barn door" (*EP*, 55), a space no one else sees. At other times and places, he also sees ghosts, even Shakespeare once.

Then, looking out the window of a room built onto his barn/bookstore, he sees a pair of feet sticking out from under the porch. Peter's grandson, Tip, "recognized them as his mother's feet, his mother's varicose veins—from bearing him, she had told him; the doctors had warned her. He recognized the straw shoes, the toes pointed and a little scuffed with pompoms on them—a witch's shoes" (*EP*, 10). Gradually, the space around Peter Ringkoping takes shape. The characters and events of *Porlock*, seen in the metaphors they embody, exist not only in Vermont but also in the Land of Oz. Like the Tin Woodman, Peter finds a heart. Like the Scarecrow, Peter's older son, Tommy, finds a brain. Like the Cowardly Lion, Peter's young son, Nels, finds courage. And like Dorothy, Peter's grandson, Tip, finds his way home. At the end of the Yellow Brick Road, in the Emerald City, Pilgrim Village, the Wizard Hans Strasser sets everything to rights.

The entire enveloping metaphor takes shape as metaphor after metaphor appears in the characters and events. They provide the outward and visible sign of the inner shape that the imagination of the reader fills in to give a total vision. It's all there in *Porlock*.

The novel in which the same thing takes place and that I find tugging hardest at my own heartstrings is *The Final Beast*. Here metaphor follows metaphor to illumine the characters and events, and they in metaphorical guise add up to the whole story. It is not, perhaps, so tidy as *Porlock*, but it has even more the smell of reality. What happens there, in the story that emerges from Buechner's experience and takes root in ours, illustrates what Buechner describes as happening in *The Brothers Karamazov*. What he says about Dostoevsky's novel might well be said, with appropriate revisions, of *The Final Beast*:

> The book could hardly be less didactic in any narrow sense. It is full of darkness and ambiguity. The characters are continually lacerating themselves and each other through their terrible pride. Ivan's devastating attack on belief in an all-powerful and loving God nearly overwhelms us as it nearly overwhelms his brother Alyosha. . . . It

teaches no easy lesson about virtue and nobility, and yet to read it as seriously as it asks to be read, and as it was written, is to emerge from it in some profound way the better for it. (*RCR*, 180)

And in the process Buechner's experience of what it is like to believe in God in such a world as ours becomes incarnated via metaphor in the characters and events and then is transmitted into our own experience with transforming power.

Then there is Leo Bebb, probably the most unforgettable of Buechner's characters. Antonio Parr meets him at the beginning of *Lion Country* and introduces us to some of the others who accompany him in the four Bebb novels.

> Halfway down the subway stairs, he turned. There was a smell of stale urine. It was raining on Lexington Avenue. . . .
>
> He said, "We'll be seeing you," and then continued on down the stairs, a fleshy, scrubbed man in a tight black raincoat with a narrow-brimmed hat, dimly Tyrolean, on the top of his head. Happy Hooligan. *We'll be seeing you.* . . .
>
> Leo Bebb. He was all by himself, and because I had only that day for the first time met him face to face, I had no way of knowing who his *we* included. But I came to know in some detail later, and when I close my eyes now and try to conjure up again that moment at the subway entrance, I don't exactly see the others on the stairs with him but I sense them waiting for him in the shadows a dozen steps or so further down. In reality they were all at that time safe, to use the word rather loosely, in Armadillo, Florida, but I nonetheless picture them waiting for Bebb there in the flatulent bowels of the IRT—Sharon, that willowy carnivore, that sleepy-limbed huntress, that hierodule; and Lucille, the mother, with her black glasses and wet, liverish lips; and Brownie with his china teeth smiling his unrelentingly seraphic smile. Bebb descends to them like Orpheus with his lyre, and in the dark they reach out their hands to him while up there at the entrance to the underworld I also reach out my hands. (*LC* in *BB*, 3)

He describes Bebb with more metaphors: "His mouth snapped shut like something on hinges, a nutcracker man's mouth or the mouth of one of those wooden bottle-stoppers carved into faces that they pour whiskey out of sometimes in bars. A workable Tweedledum mouth with the lines at the corners, the hinge marks, making an almost perfect H with the tight lips" (*LC* in *BB*, 4).

"What was there about Bebb that engaged me so?" Buechner asks and answers

> Bebb appears in the opening scene of *Lion Country* about to head down a flight of subway stairs, and in a way it was down into just such a subterranean dusk that I followed him, except that here I must change the metaphor because where Bebb was, it was rarely dusk. It was dusk, rather, that I left behind in following him.
> Where Bebb was, the Florida sunshine was—the hot, bright sun that the lions in the cageless zoo of Lion Country dozed and coupled in, that shone down blindingly on Bebb no less when he did whatever he did in front of the children in Miami Beach than when just possibly he raised his old friend Brownie from the dead in Knoxville, Tennessee. Bebb was strong in most of the places where I was weak, and mad as a hatter in most of the places where I was all too sane. Bebb took terrible risks with his life where I hung back with mine and hoped no one would notice. In more ways than literally, Bebb was continually exposing himself, coming right out and telling it the way it was, let the chips fall where they might, whereas I spent hours by myself every day trying to tell it exactly right and telling other people's stories rather than my own. Bebb's doubts were darker and more painful than mine because he had grown up knowing more of pain and darkness, and that made his faith both a kind of crazy miracle in itself and a faith also that could work miracles. (*NT*, 99–100)

Then, in contrast with Bebb, there is the ex-husband of Antonio's dying sister Miriam. His name is Charlie Blaine, dead in the midst of his own life.

> The man's a bleeding ghost. . . . Do you know what I *mean* when I say he sleeps most of the time? I mean he often doesn't get up till noon, and when he naps, he doesn't just nap when it's raining or something but right in the middle of a sunny afternoon, for God's sake, with the kids and me roaming around in bathing suits right under his window. Sleep's his escape from life, Tono. Some-

day, they'll have to come wake him up and tell him he's dead. (*LC* in *BB*, 21–22)

It is not only in the novels that the metaphors flow like good wine or like blood in a life-giving transfusion. In his Beecher Lectures at Yale, Buechner begins with Henry Ward Beecher—looking at his face in the mirror just before he must go to give those same lectures in 1872:

So when he stood there looking at himself in the hotel mirror with soap on his face and a razor in his hand, part of what he saw was his own shame and horror, the sight of his own folly, the judgment one can imagine he found even harder to bear than God's, which was his own judgment on himself, because whereas God is merciful, we are none of us very good at showing mercy on ourselves. Henry Ward Beecher cut himself with his razor and wrote out notes for that first Beecher Lecture in blood, because, whatever else he was or aspired to be or was famous for being, he was a man of flesh and blood, and so were all the men who over the years traveled to New Haven after him to deliver the same lectures. (*TT*, 2)

In *A Long Day's Dying*, there is the character George Motley, the novelist who gives a lecture at Princeton. In his talk he comments on the way a writer works with characters and events to project meaning. He tells a story:

"Now it seems there was a rabble-rouser once, an anarchist if you will, who was in the habit of taking his tea in one of those parks where anarchy and the like are the subjects of much extemporaneous oratory. Well, one day as he sat there, on his favorite red bench, a heretofore inoffensive bird sprang up nearby and, as it flew above the anarchist, released a soupçon or two of droppings on his head and then flew off again. Our friend examined the damage to his ensemble, shook a heavy, guttural fist at the retreating bird, and snarled angrily: 'For the rich you sing!'" (*LDD*, 78–79)

Motley points out that one could change the entire fabric of the story by changing the anarchist into "an unsuccessful writer, or at least a young and struggling one, and let us say that what he curses are the successful writers whom he considers inferior" (*LDD*, 79). What he is really saying is that with the right opportunities, if the bird gave him its song, he too could use it to become successful. But, asks Motley, what can we tell him?

> "Why, we can tell him that he can make something out of what the bird did give him, I mean that from the bird, the symbol of his personal experience, he can—with the help of imagination—distill as much as others can from what is perhaps a richer experience. . . . From this story, as a story and not a parable, it is possible to fashion anything from a Divine Comedy to a short story in any one of the *hausfrau* magazines." (*LDD*, 80)

On one level Motley is suggesting, and perhaps Buechner through him, that writers must take their own experience and transform it into art. On another level what is being said is that characters and events in a story convey meaning in metaphorical form. Changing the metaphors embodied in the characters and events alters the entire fabric of meaning. On still another level Motley may himself be an embodied metaphor who, in telling this story as well as in his actions in the novel, represents that variegated, ambiguous element in experience, even as his name suggests.

In *The Seasons' Difference*, Peter Cowley, the teacher who thinks he had a religious vision, is a real person in the novel who functions metaphorically as the responsiveness in humanity to the spiritual, which contains both threat and promise. In *The Return of Ansel Gibbs*, Gibbs himself acts out a pattern that pervades human experience—that of the dedicated, insensitive public servant who can do much good and harm to others, yet can be jarred by events toward greater awareness and humanity. Dr. Kuykendall, on the other hand, embodies a metaphor of passionate involvement with, and commitment to, those in suffering and need.

With Dostoevsky, Buechner turns each of his novels into one enveloping metaphor. The "return" of Ansel Gibbs is much more than his coming back from his retirement to public life. He returns to contact with his old professor who had inspired him, and returns to the experience of his friend's suicide through meeting the friend's son. Through these "returns," he turns again toward a humanity he had lost. Out of the crisis of returning to his past comes a *metanoia*, a turning toward a renewed depth of meaning and faith.

The Final Beast also is a single metaphor drawn from Stephen Crane's poem "The Black Riders," in which monsters wrangle over the world: "But of all the sadness this was sad— / A woman's arms tried to shield / The head of a sleeping man / From the jaws of the final beast." The metaphor of *The Entrance to Porlock* is a journey—in search of wholeness through life, toward death, and beyond.

> As for *Lion Country*, Bebb says it better than I can: Antonio, you take a man's been in prison a couple years, and he's ready for Jesus like he's never been ready any place else. He's ready for anything has got some hope and life in it. Life, Antonio, is what a prisoner's ready for. Freedom. Lion Country. It's worth breaking the law just so you can get put in the lock-up, where the grapes are ripe for the harvest and the Lord needs all the hands he can get for the vineyard. You should hear the way they sing hymns behind bars, Antonio. Makes you go all over gooseflesh. (*LC* in *BB*, 114)

It's the same for *Open Heart*, *Love Feast*, *Treasure Hunt*, and *Godric*. Leaves, leaves, leaves, and the tree—metaphors and metaphors merge in one metaphor that points toward God with a too-good-not-to-be-true faith.

In the Bible there are also characters and events. The book of the Exodus tells of the oppression of the Hebrews in Egypt, of the call to Moses in the burning bush, and of the Hebrews leaving Egypt under Moses' leadership. It makes an interesting story. But in the telling and retelling within the long Hebrew tradition, the events of exodus and escape become more than an account of what happened long ago. The story points beyond itself to the power of God, God's continuing governance of history, and God's liberation of those who are oppressed. Metaphor added to metaphor calls down the centuries.

Something similar happens in Buechner's writings, as he suggests it does also in Dostoevsky's. Vivid characters and events occur and reoccur. Then, before our eyes and within our hearts, we find ourselves dwelling in Buechner's weird and wonderful world of faith. A penny drops. A light dawns. We understand ourselves and our companions in a new way.

IMAGES AND SYMBOLS

"The preaching of the Gospel," Buechner says in his Beecher Lectures, "is a telling of the truth or the putting of a sort of frame of words around the silence that is truth because truth in the sense of fullness, of the way things are, can at best be only pointed to by the language of poetry—of metaphor, image, symbol—as it is used in the prophets of the Old Testament and elsewhere" (*TT*, 25). That is what he is doing, this master of prose who uses the language of poetry to paint his pictures: he is pointing to God with images and symbols gift-wrapped in metaphors.

The images that appear again and again in Buechner's writing are, for the most part, familiar to us. Many of them emerge from the ordinary experiences that he sees are bearers of truth, the embodiment especially of *our* truths. Just possibly they can become for us the incarnation of the holy.

In *The Entrance to Porlock*, there is a passage that fascinates me. Hans Strasser, the director of Pilgrim Village, gets the retarded adults who live there together in the auditorium while Peter Ringkoping and family are visiting. On the stage he places a large, blank bulletin board and a carton of cloth scraps. He asks everyone to speak of an experience they have had that day. Hands go up. One person mentions the lawn getting mowed. Hans takes a green swatch from the box and pins it on the board. As each person speaks he adds more pieces: "Yellow, green, cream, lavender, rose—flame blue and crimson—some pinned flat, some hanging in folds overlapping others like scales" (*EP*, 237). Then he asks one villager to name the collage. The boy first stutters uncertainly and then says, "Today. Its name is Today." "That is a good name," Strasser said. . . . "Arthur, thank you for naming it. It is a good name. It is the flag of our day together, and we salute it because it is holy and because it is ours" (*EP*, 239).

Buechner's recurring images will be especially familiar to those who know well the biblical Christian tradition. But the way he uses what is well known may surprise or even shock us. Pilate waiting for an unimportant, provincial Messiah to be brought before him is depicted as a modern, harassed executive trying to maintain his position in a competitive organization long enough to retire respectably and comfortably. Bebb as dirty old man exposing himself becomes a means of grace who discloses to us that we must all stand exposed before each other and God.

By juxtaposing seemingly contradictory images, Buechner changes completely the way we look at images and ourselves. He does this in a fashion that sets us off on paths of association that widen our awareness, compels us to recall elements of our own experience that we may have forgotten or have wanted to forget, and places us in an unanticipated relation to those questions that haunt the horizons of life.

As the images recur and take on enlarged meaning in relation to one another and to the nagging doubts and depths of our own experience, images such as the individual swatches of cloth on Hans Strasser's bulletin board gradually merge and become transformed into symbol. No longer is our ordinary experience unimportant nor can we express our faith in hackneyed, theological abstractions on Sunday. Images transmuted through Buechner's artistry into symbols become night lights of faith, giving us courage to dwell in the dark times of uncertainty and tragedy because we know we are home.

Turning lead into gold seems simple when compared with the impossible magic Buechner proposes to work as he rolls up his sleeves, shows us hands with nothing more in them than we find in the emptiness of our own palms, and starts out on his story. As we look at the images he places before us and witness their transmutations, we glimpse the magic of his artistry even if we do not grasp the sleight of hand by which, as in an act of medieval alchemy, images become symbols of faith.

My own list of images is long, but it could easily be longer, and Buechner buffs may complain that I have omitted important ones. I can only encourage readers to use my list as a point of departure. As you read Buechner and are drawn into his spell, make your own list.

My list of key images in Buechner's writing includes those on the accompanying table.

KEY IMAGES IN BUECHNER'S WRITING

Death	Feet	Laughter	Secrets
Dreams	Fire	Limelight	Shit/Sin
Expectancy	Foolishness	Loneliness	Silence
Faces	Home	Names	Time
Fairy Tales	Jesus' Coming	Paradox	Waiting
Faith	Journey		

Here I shall discuss only a few images that seem especially important and that I have not written much about elsewhere.

Faces. This image turns up again and again throughout Buechner's writing. In *The Faces of Jesus*, Buechner points out how the character of the human visage incarnates the divine:

> He had a face. . . .
> . . .He was a man once, whatever else he may have been. And he had a man's face, a human face. . . . Like you and me he had a face his life gave shape to and that shaped his life and others's lives, and with part of ourselves I think we might turn away from the mystery of that face, that life, as much of the time we turn away from the mystery of life itself. With part of ourselves I think we might avoid meeting his real eyes, if such a meeting were possible, the way at certain moments we avoid meeting our own real eyes in mirrors because for better or worse they threaten to tell us more than we want to know. (*FJ*, 9)

And at the end of that book he writes:

> The face of Jesus is a face that belongs to us the way our past belongs to us. It is a face that we belong to if only as to the one face out of the past that has perhaps had more to do with the shaping of our present than any other. According to Paul, the face of Jesus is our own face finally, the face we will all come to look like a little when the kingdom comes and we are truly ourselves at last, truly the brothers and sisters of one another and the children of God. (*FJ*, 240)

Whereas the face of Jesus gives meaning, human faces without faith are lost in confusion. In one of the sermons included in *The Hungering Dark*, Buechner focuses on peculiar words from the book of Daniel: "To us belongs confusion of face."

> It is a strange phrase, but it is also a just one. Confusion of face is somehow the truth of it. Because faces are confusing, that is all. The preacher looks out at the faces of his congregation, and he is confused. He sees expressions in those faces of attention and inattention, of vague expectancy and glazed resignation, and he wonders what is going on behind those faces. . . . And to go just one step further . . . he is often confused by his own face, and he would

not be likely to admit this if he were not quite certain that all men are often confused by their own faces too. (*HD*, 18)

Daniel identifies confusion of face with turning aside from the commandments of God and acting wickedly. Buechner too, in his own way, uses the image to point to sin. Confusion of face becomes, in his hands, the face as facade behind which we hide from ourselves, from others, and from God. Each of us, whether we are looking into the faces of others or looking at the reflection of our own face in the mirror, tends toward confusion of human face.

But confusion is not the only possibility in the plurality of faces, Buechner suggests, speaking of Jesus:

> To say he had a face is to say that like the rest of us he had many faces as the writers of the Old Testament knew who used the Hebrew word almost exclusively in its plural form. To their way of thinking, the face of man is not a front for him to live his life behind but a frontier, the outermost, visible edge of his life itself in all its richness and multiplicity, and hence they spoke not of the face of a man or of God but of his faces. The *faces* of Jesus then—all the ways he had of being and of being seen. (*FJ*, 10)

The image of face, therefore, draws us into a journey across the frontier of our emerging possibilities in God.

Journey. Our confrontation with our own faces and the faces of others results in confusion, and that confusion takes us on a journey into ourselves and perhaps into new territory filled with meaning. Buechner tells us of his own journey, and we discover that it has taken him toward deeper levels of faith and understanding and has become for him a sacred journey. That journey has taken him to the face and the faces of Jesus Christ, in whom he sees the reality of the true self of each of us revealed.

> The voyage into the self is long and dark and full of peril, but I believe that it is a voyage that all of us will have to make before we are through. Either we climb down into the abyss willingly with our eyes open, or we risk falling into it with our eyes closed—a point on which religion and psychiatry seem to agree. And I believe that what is said in the language of the Japanese poem is true also

in the language of fact; that if we search ourselves deeply enough, we will begin to see at last who we really are, we will begin to see, very dimly at first, our own true faces. And then, although on the surface the fever may rage still, I believe that a strange calm does begin to come, a peace that passes understanding.

. . . And whatever your religion is, or your lack of religion, in this sense I think that the soul of every man is Christian and that the man on the cross who finds peace and fullness and true life is at the very least a symbol of the deepest truth about every one of us. I believe that by God's grace it is our destiny, in this life or in whatever life awaits us, to discover the face of our inmost being, to become at last and at great cost who we truly are. (*HD*, 23)

In Buechner's view the very word *religion* directs our attention to those times when we stumble in our experience upon what we cannot understand, and discover in the mystery of it all "a summons to pilgrimage, a come-all-ye," where we are "led to suspect the reality of splendors" beyond our ability to name; where we discern "meanings no less overwhelming because they can only be hinted at in myths and rituals, in foolish, left-handed games and cloudy novels; where in great laughter" we glimpse a destination for our journey that we shall never comprehend fully until we arrive at the end of our travels (*AG*, 75).

Death. In this way the images of face and journey take us inescapably toward that earthly ending of life that is called death. Yet only as we are able to endure the voyage that includes not only death as we experience it in general and in others, but also *our own death*, can we hope to arrive where, in the deepest recesses of ourselves, we long to be.

Among the images present in Buechner's writing, few are more pervasive than death. It has a variety of forms — physical death, spiritual death, being dead in life, the act of suicide, accidental death, death as a taboo that can be used for grisly humor or for shock effect.

In *Lion Country* Antonio's twin sister, Miriam, lies dying in a New York hospital. She has a form of cancer which makes her increasingly fragile as the disease progresses, so that toward the end she breaks a bone in her arm as she reaches for a glass of water. Death has permeated her whole life and her entire body. She has reached the point where her dying is the only vocation left to her. "'It's like having a baby,' Miriam said. 'Only the baby I'm going to have is me'" (*LC* in *BB*, 8). To accomplish that one purpose, she had gradually withdrawn herself from everyone and everything in the world around her. Death has an increasingly antiseptic quality. As she gives birth to herself, it means no longer touching and no longer being touched by the old life around her.

Death can also permeate the living of those who are in a medical sense thoroughly alive. Brownie, slipping his life under his rear end and sitting on it, is dead, and Bebb, who has so much vitality that he not only risks exposing it but seems compelled to do so, is life. And there is pale, pious Reginald, who compares with old Godric—remembering his boisterous, roistering youth as well as his equally energetic commitment to the hermit's life and to God—as death compares with life.

Death also means our own death, as Antonio discovers. The day after learning about the sexual involvement of his wife, Sharon, with his nephew Tony, to avoid facing Sharon, Antonio goes to New York and visits Miriam's grave:

> I was still standing there in this kind of empty-headed trance, and then it was like what happens when, just as you're about to go to sleep at night, you seem to trip over something and can feel the whole bed shake under you. . . . And just at that instant of being brought back to myself I knew that the self I'd been brought back to was some fine day going to be as dead as Miriam. I knew it not just in the usual sense of knowing but knew it in almost the Biblical sense of having sex with it. I knew I didn't just *have* a body. I *was* a body. It was like walking into a closed door at night. The thud jolted me down to the roots of my hair.
>
> The body I was was going to be dead. Through Sharon and Tony I'd finally come to believe it, but through grace alone I banged right into it—not a lesson this time, a collision. (*OH* in *BB*, 197)

Names. When there is a lump in the throat, and the mystery at the core of our lives calls us on our separate journeys, which are somehow one in God, then the need for words arises. We need to name what we have experienced, not because the naming can ever be a substitute for the reality or because we think that the reality cannot happen without the words, but rather because we need words to express what has happened to us, to know what it has been, to fix it in our minds, to communicate it to others, and to be able to call it back up for ourselves.

It is a kind of magic, a spell that letters spelling out a name can cast upon us for good or ill:

"In the name of Jesus Christ," I pray and then what? "Let me fall into no sin this day nor run into any kind of danger," I pray. The Lord Jesus Christ and the power of his name. Jesus. The power of any name, spoken, clack-clack, at the fulness of time to break your heart or rejoice your heart. Both maybe. All the invisibleness of a life made manifest in the visible name. (*AG*, 78)

But it is not only a magic that belongs to words uttered in ecclesiastical settings. Names have the power to call up those ranges of ordinary experience that have within them the potential depth of meaning and pain and love.

My father's name where to say goodbye he wrote it in pencil on the last page of the last book, *Gone with the Wind*, that he read, and all the mystery in this signature of his wandering from job to job after the apotheosis of college, his astonishment at discovering, he who had been a guest all his life and life his host, that when troubles forced him home, he of all people had nowhere to go home to. (*AG*, 78–79)

Into that fullness of life that words can take us comes something more. We find ourselves confronted not only with the ordinary but also with the extraordinary that goes with it, often in most unlikely places. And the depth of life becomes religious.

The name of a friend coming up in the conversation of a stranger so that the friend is suddenly there in the stranger's face. The name of someone you once were in love with. The name that in certain places, at certain times, it would be unbearable to name. The name of places: Auschwitz and Roncevalles, Hamburg Hill, Versailles, Antietam, Montgomery, Camelot, Bethlehem, Cambridge. The sound of your own name on somebody else's lips. Shouted down from a window, called out from a crowd of faces, the power that your name has to make you turn, to make you hear, to make you answer, to make you *be* your name. Yahweh telling Moses his name so that Moses could make God turn and be. Your own secret name written on a white stone and known only to you when at last you receive it. (*AG*, 79)

We meet God, that final reality and meaning that reveals to us our own real name and our own destiny.

Silence. Buechner tells of a time when he spent several days at an Episcopal monastery on the Hudson River north of New York. He went there in the hopes of getting answers to some of the questions of his life. He had heard especially of one monk who, he had been told, would be especially helpful. When Buechner arrived, ready to ask his questions and receive answers from the holy father, he learned that the man was in retreat and seeing no one. Rather than answers, Buechner encountered silence. "I discovered," he writes,

> that all the other fathers and brothers observed what they called the Great Silence so that they couldn't even say good morning when they met you in the corridors but only nodded and smiled as though they knew some joke too rich to tell. Lastly I discovered that the one father whose job it was to speak to visitors was willing to tackle any question I put to him but that a stroke had left his speech so impaired that his words ran together like raindrops on a windowpane and I could understand almost nothing of what he said. So for two or three days I had nothing but silence to listen to—a silence broken mainly, as I remember it, by the sound of rapping on wood strangely enough: the rapping on the door of my cell at daybreak and the muffled cry from the hallway of *Christ is risen*; the abbot rapping on the refectory table to signal the end of our silent meals; the rap-tapping of sandaled feet down the silent corridors. None of the questions I had come with was answered except as the silence was answer, and the answer of the silence, as I understood it, was that I should myself be silent, which I was, so silent that after awhile, at least for a time, even my questions were silenced. (*AG*, 45–46)

And there is the silence in church on a Sunday as the sermon is about to begin. Here is silence pregnant with possibilities. Preachers may say something that will be for someone the truth or they may fall right out of the pulpit onto their faces or onto some other part of their anatomies before God and the congregation. But Buechner knows that the silence is more than emptiness: it is the expectancy of waiting for the preacher to say something that moves us and calls us to believe.

There is also the silence *before* God and the silence *of* God.

Before the Gospel is a word, it is silence. . . .

Out of the silence let the only real news come, which is sad news before it is glad news and that is fairy tale last of all. Preachers are not brave enough to be literally silent for long, and since it is their calling to speak the truth with love, even if they were brave enough, they would not be silent for long because we are none of us very good at silence. It says too much. So let them use words, but, in addition to using them to explain, expound, exhort, let them use them to evoke, to set us dreaming as well as thinking, to use words as at their most prophetic and truthful, the prophets used them to stir in us memories and longings and intuitions that we starve for without knowing that we starve. Let them use words which do not only try to give answers to the questions that we ask or ought to ask but which help us to hear the questions that we do not have words for asking and to hear the silence that those questions rise out of and the silence that is the answer to those questions. (*TT*, 23–24)

Shit/Sin. In *The Final Beast* the young minister, Nicolet, trying to get to a parishioner in trouble, is caught in a rainstorm while hitchhiking and picked up by a boy in a car. In the course of their conversation, the boy asks him why he became a minister. By way of response Nicolet wanders into a story about a beer-drinking friend in college who seemed preoccupied with four-letter words.

> "Eats it," Nicolet said. "The great fecal indictment. It's all he could say. I suppose I should have been able to see what was coming next, but I didn't. We'd gotten on religion, I told you. Well, he suddenly said a memorable thing, an epic thing—at least it was to me. . . . According to him, Christ eats it too."
>
> . . . "At the time it knocked me for a loop even though I must have been half tight myself. But it was step one, the voice in the burning bush all right whether it sounded much like it then or not. Much later I realized my drinking companion had spoken the truth. Christ does eat it, or course. You know why?"
>
> The boy shook his head.
>
> "Because it's all this world has ever given him to eat. And yet he keeps coming back for more." (*FB*, 82–83)

As a reason to enter the ministry, it may sound strange. But it is as right as the rain that drenched Nicolet, so right that it brings tears to my eyes every time I read it. It takes me back to my teens, when my family lived in a dreary trailer park, supposedly the biggest trailer park in the entire country, because my father was working on a nearby construction project. There was a Methodist minister who endured the heat and the dust to keep an interdenominational church going, and every summer two or three interns from seminary came to work with him. I wondered why they would give up all the other places they could be and all the other things they could be doing in order to spend their time with the people living in that seemingly Godforsaken collection of trailers. When I found the answer, just as Buechner did, I went to college and then to seminary, called out of myself and perhaps out of my right mind by a God shown to me by that minister and those seminary interns, a God who takes on the worst of the world, is crucified, and comes back for more.

Buechner doesn't let go of the theme. Near the end of *The Final Beast*, Irma Reinwasser, Nicolet's housekeeper, is burned to death in a prank when some boys try to lure her into stamping out a fire with a bag of shit in the middle of it that they have set outside her door (*FB*, 260–2).

In *Open Heart* Leo Bebb says, "Sin is waste, Antonio. Sin is life wasted" (*OH*, *BB*, 147). Perhaps that is closely akin to the places where he equates shit with sin. In *Love Feast* he offers a discourse of astonishing proportions on the subject. Professor Virgil Roebuck is attempting to get Bebb's love feasts thrown off the Princeton campus. A meeting takes place between them when Bebb goes to Roebuck's office to protest the eviction. The subject is shit, as Bebb recounts it later to Antonio. Roebuck had told Bebb you didn't have to be an expert psychologist to explain Bebb's trick eyelid.

> "He said that eyelid was a dead giveaway how the only way a man like me can go on believing in Almighty God is by pulling that eyelid down like a window blind between me and all the shit in the world that proves there isn't any Almighty God and never was or will be.
> "You take a word like shit, Antonio. A preacher isn't even supposed to know there is those kind of words, and Roebuck, he thought he'd throw me a curve just using it. I said, 'Roebuck, you think I don't know about shit? What you've been telling me about

isn't even a millionth part of all the shit there is because you've stuck to just the religious shit, and that's only one kind of all there is because piled up right alongside it there's a million other kinds.' . . . I used that word shit to him till it begun to sound like I invented it.

. . . "Antonio, shit is what preachers have been talking about since Moses except the word they're more like to use is sin." (*LF* in *BB*, 351–2)

But Bebb saw deeper into Roebuck's vendetta against God. All the professor's talk about God's nonexistence was really a way of expressing his grief for his disabled son who could not use his hands or feet. "That's the main shit the world tossed in your direction, isn't it Roebuck?" Bebb asks (*LF* in *BB*, 352).

"Antonio, I busted in there mad as a hornet, but you can't stay mad when you start thinking things like that. . . .

"I said, 'Virgil, the night is dark, and we are far from home. . . . The night is dark, Virgil Roebuck, and home's a long ways off for both of us.' . . .

"Antonio, we're far from home, all of us are. Who's going to judge which of us has got the farthest way to go through all the shit and the dark?" (*LF* in *BB*, 353)

In such passages as these, Buechner is calling us to rethink those parts of our lives that we usually do not want to talk about because we think them somehow not nice and possibly even beyond the care and concern of the Creator. God's grace, Buechner suggests, just may be there waiting for us in those dirty, obscene, and seemingly Godforsaken sectors of our lives.

Jesus' Coming. This is an image that is fun and wonderful to explore, because of the guises in which it happens. There is the "clack-clack" of the apple branches that, for the young minister Nicolet, means "the approach of the approach perhaps of splendor." But Buechner also has more playfully serious forms for the coming of Jesus. The Lone Ranger is a Christ figure, "riding into the world with justice on one hip and mercy on the other" (*TH* in *BB*, 516). And so is Mr. Keen, Tracer of Lost Persons. Jesus comes too through other people. "I wait for my friend . . . and it is on my friend that what I become next depends. . . . We are in each other's hands. . . . Who knows in what partial way the long expected one appears, in what disguise the one who is to come comes" (*AG*, 102–3).

But *be not affeard*, says Caliban, nor is he the only one to say it. "Be not afraid," says another, "for lo, I am with you always, even unto the end of the world." He says he is with us on our journeys. He says he has been with us since each of our journeys began. Listen for him. Listen to the sweet and bitter airs of your present and your past for the sound of him. (*SJ*, 78)

And so the images Buechner uses go on in a rich procession that joins an endless line of splendor. The pictures become vivid images, and the images perhaps grow into symbols. What appears on the periphery of Buechner's vision becomes central, because he transforms the edges of perception into the frame that defines the picture, and the lost comes into focus and is found.

THE METAPHYSICS OF IRONY

In *Treasure Hunt*, Brownie arrives in Poinsett, South Carolina, from Texas. To the surprise of Antonio and Sharon, Brownie, who they thought never drank, is definitely tipsy when he gets off the plane. Sharon says, "Listen, Bip always said flying scared the piss out of him too. If a couple of belts help, why not?" (*TH* in *BB*, 453). But what has driven Brownie to the bottle is not fear of flying. It's something, in his view, worse. He has lost his faith and nothing matters anymore. "Oh, I'm not scared of flying, dear," he says. "That's not the problem. When life doesn't mean much to you any more, death doesn't mean so much either" (*TH* in *BB*, 453).

Brownie the nondrinker drinks. The meaning of life gives death its meaning. Buechner's characters appear before us clothed in contradictory metaphors. The effect is to provide a twist of irony to flavor every flagon filled with images. Not only is the metaphor itself a way of getting an odd-angled perspective on the subject, but the metaphors used provide a contrast that heightens the already implicit irony and gives a slightly crazy, schizoid view of the world. Antonio reflects: "Sharon and I had both of us experienced more or less the same thing. It is when the public world begins to pull into two like the private one that the real nightmare starts. Irony is another word for it, I suppose—the good turning out to be bad, the real the unreal" (*TH* in *BB*, 454).

Out of the experience of this split comes a fascinating understanding of metaphor: "the grim metaphysics of irony, the helpless babbling in the presence of the unspeakable that is metaphor" (*TH* in *BB*, 462). Metaphor is not only a literary device that writers use to throw light on the known from the vantage point of their wider knowledge; metaphor is also evoked by the contradictions and pain of living, drawn from the writer as a dentist pulls teeth. It is also an attempt to deal with the symbolic dimensions of experience that demands meanings when it is not clear that meaning is there. So literature picks up the bits and pieces that writers have available to them and seeks by means of metaphor piled upon metaphor to wrest some shred of significance from the crosscurrents of irony around us.

Antonio muses at one point in *Treasure Hunt* on irony:

> I have read that men shot down in battle who've lived to tell the tale tell that there comes a moment when you rise high in the air above your own body and look down at where it lies on the ground as good as dead. . . .
>
> I have looked at my sister in a hospital with storm-tinted windows and both legs in casts with a bar betweeen them so she is a white A on a white bed. . . .
>
> I have looked at Stephen Kulak who sits in my ninth grade class as I explain what irony is. It is saying one thing and meaning another thing, I say—two things. That doesn't give him any trouble but the idea that life can be ironic too does; so out of my Santa's pack I pull the example of a bride getting killed on her way to a wedding. En route to a fresh start she runs into a dead-end—two things—and in a classroom with the Pledge of Allegiance on the walls and Christmas scotchtaped to the windows I look at Stephen Kulak's face falling like Rome to the barbarians. He knows what irony is. (*TH*, 216–7)

In an ironic turn of Buechner's theo-logic, good and evil do not cancel each other out but add up to grace. The worst thing is not the last. Even the worst can be redeemed, may even become a means of redemption. And God becomes incarnate in a crucified hick from Galilee.

The most delicate irony of all may be faith itself—"to be going and not know why. . . . To have as having not, to grasp nothing but always to hold in the open palm of your hand" (*FB*, 45). And if faith is not the greatest irony of all, then surely God is!

Nowhere does Buechner's "metaphysics of irony" hit me harder than at the close of *The Final Beast*, in a passage illustrating the fascinating point that Buechner refuses to create a totally evil character. Nicolet and a few friends are standing at Irma Reinwasser's grave with raindrops beginning to fall. He is about to begin the service of committal. The cemetery is on a narrow spit of land that seems to Nicolet the prow of a ship on which they are waiting. "Nothing that he could see was as real as the sense of sailing on a ship that he could not see, and he could feel the earth tilt beneath his feet with the grey swells, the raindrops flicking his hands and face like sea-spray." Then he notices that Poteat, the editor who had caused the trouble leading to Irma's death, had joined the small group around the grave. This is the Poteat who, when his attempt to cause a scandal had failed, had hidden himself in his house to avoid facing Nicolet; the Poteat, I might add, who had shoved his life even further under his tail than had Brownie. Poteat's presence itself did not surprise Nicolet.

> Only what he could not see seemed capable now of surprising him, whatever it might be, whatever secret the voyage held. He found that he was glad that Poteat had come—not Poteat as he actually saw him there, dabbing under his chin with his white handkerchief, but Poteat as no one saw him, Poteat as he was not and as he might become or might never become. The thunder sounded farther away, but the sky darkened.
>
> "And I saw the heavens opened," Nicolet began to read, "and behold a white horse, and he that sat upon him was called Faithful and True, and in righteousness he doth judge and make war." And *I wish you well*, he thought, as if this itself was the secret, *I wish you well, I wish you well*. Nicolet glanced up at them, squinted at them, voyagers with him, through the drizzle. (*FB*, 273–4)

Poteat starts aways when the service is over and then comes back and puts his hand on Nicolet's shoulder.

> "Good show, pal," he said. The dimples were like black slits in his face, like gills, as he smiled. "Just one little thing. This supper

of the great God . . . no more death, no more pain. Ask her." He pointed down to the ground. "The Hell you say, pal. The Hell you say." He made a quick jab with one finger to tickle the stomach of Lizzie, who had come close with her sister to watch. They both darted back, giggling, and then they did an unexpected thing.

They grabbed up some flowers that they had brought and started pelting him with them—orange hawkweed, daisies, clover—and stooping over like a great, pale bear in his baggy seersucker suit, he kept on lunging at them with his finger. Nicolet, Bluebeard, threw back his head and laughed. Even old Roy had to smile as Poteat went lumbering off with the little girls after him. When he got as far as Nicolet's car, he turned around for a moment, and it was only then that they could see that he was more or less laughing himself. (*FB*, 276)

"If literature is a metaphor for the writer's experience," Buechner writes, "a mirror in which that experience is at least partially reflected, it is at the same time a mirror in which the reader can also see his or her experience reflected in a new and potentially transforming way" (*RCR*, 180). We do not get academic proofs that convince us of God's existence, but we may just possibly find ourselves caught up in a deeper sense of human feeling in faith and hope and love. That is all we have a right to expect. That is more than enough.

CHAPTER 7

Dwelling in Buechner's Worlds:
Life Itself is Grace

When I enter the world of Buechner's novels, I feel as though I am living in them and living through them. Each of the characters becomes a facet of myself — to be worried over, laughed at, judged, cleansed, and returned to its place as part of me — and I find that I am somewhat better reconciled with all my selves than before. As I am drawn into the locations and situations of his stories, I come to dwell in the reality Buechner creates around me, and within that reality I discover above all that I live in a world filled with grace.

This "dwelling in," to use Michael Polanyi's phrase again, amounts to an experience of identification with Buechner's characters. Godric, the unlikely saint of the twelfth century, dies saying, "All's lost. All's found. Farewell." And my tears flow for myself no less than for Godric. Hans Strasser in *The Entrance to Porlock* murmurs to the child/man Tommy, who holds off what he fears by making jokes, "We do not forget you. We love you too, Mr. Tommy." And I feel understood and forgiven. In *Love Feast* Leo Bebb, the maybe charlatan/maybe saint, raises his paper cup of Tropicana punch to his flock, calling out, "Here's to Jesus, here's to you." And all the times I've participated in Communion services with others, eating bread and drinking wine or grape juice, flood in upon me, and those experiences are suddenly bathed in a new, wonderfully slanted light. After Bebb dies, Gertrude Conover (who claims she and Bebb knew each other through various incarnations) utters her memorable tribute to him, "Leo Bebb was always good company." And the feeling overwhelms me that I'd like those words used as my own epitaph. I truly *dwell in* those characters. At times I even begin to talk like them. When someone asks me a question that I don't know the answer to or feel uncertain about, I respond with the words of Leo Bebb's maybe insane/maybe sane wife, Lucille: "You tell me!" For me, that says it all.

This powerful sense of indwelling carries over from reading Buechner's stories into my reading of the Bible, and those stories become not tales of a distant time and strange world, but rather my own story as well. With Moses at the burning bush, I find myself wanting to get God pinned down with a name so I can call up the divine when I have need and so perhaps I can stave off God's sending me away on new missions. I stand among the people of Israel at Shechem and hear Joshua commanding us: "Choose ye this day whom you will serve." Jesus' story of the Good Samaritan draws me into it in the same way. When I was younger I was the strong one who helped the wounded traveler. As I became older and became busy with many responsibilities, I identified more with the priest and the Levite hurrying by on the other side to attend a meeting calling for more police to protect people on the Jericho road. And more often now I may dwell in the character who is beset by that old thief Time and left half-dead beside the road.

As this world of the Bible becomes less strange and I inhabit it as my own, the words of Buechner about the truth of the Gospel take on meaning and urgency for me. He writes:

> Let the preacher tell the truth. Let him make audible the silence of the news of the world with the sound turned off so that in that silence we can hear the tragic truth of the Gospel, which is that the world where God is absent is a dark and echoing emptiness; and the comic truth of the Gospel, which is that it is into the depths of his absence that God makes himself present in such unlikely ways and to such unlikely people that old Sarah and Abraham and maybe when the time comes even Pilate and Job and Lear and Henry Ward Beecher and you and I laugh till the tears run down our cheeks. And finally let him preach this overwhelming of tragedy by comedy, of darkness by light, of the ordinary by the extraordinary, as the tale that is too good not to be true because to dismiss it as untrue is to dismiss along with it "that catch of the breath, [that] beat and lifting of the heart near to (or even accompanied by) tears," which I believe is the deepest intuition of truth that we have. (*TT,* 98; the words in quotes are from J. R. R. Tolkien)

Many such possibilities emerge for those of us who do come to dwell in Buechner's work and his various worlds. What happens, for one thing, I am convinced, is that the more I dwell in the experiences Buechner draws me into with his magical powers as storyteller—the encounters with God made flesh, the tales drawn from his life that reach into mine—the more I am able to break out toward new insight within the world of my own life. In this way Buechner enables his readers to fill their own lives with more life. To be aware of what moves us, gives us anxiety or hope, what makes us laugh and feel alive—these are the things that put us in touch not only with ourselves but also with the places where God speaks to *us* and gives the dimension of depth to our faith.

To put it that way, however, reminds me of something that Buechner continues to affirm: life itself is *grace*. We are not able to dwell in events and make them have meaning nor break out toward new meaning solely of our own powers. The ability to find meaning, to discover that the journey itself is our home—these *are given* to us. They are grace, gracefully gracing our lives.

Grace is something you can never get but only be given. There's no way to earn it or deserve it or bring it about any more than you can deserve the taste of raspberries and cream or earn good looks or bring about your own birth.

A good sleep is grace and so are good dreams. Most tears are grace. The smell of rain is grace. Somebody loving you is grace. Loving somebody is grace. Have you ever *tried* to love somebody?

A crucial eccentricity of the Christian faith is the assertion that people are saved by grace. There's nothing *you* have to do. There's nothing you *have* to do. There's nothing you have to *do.*

The grace of God means something like: Here is your life. You might never have been, but you *are* because the party wouldn't have been complete without you. Here is the world. Beautiful and terrible things will happen. Don't be afraid. I am with you. Nothing can ever separate us. It's for you I created the universe. I love you.

There's only one catch. Like any other gift, the gift of grace can be yours only if you'll reach out and take it.

Maybe being able to reach out and take it is a gift too. (*WT*, 33–34)

In a way that this passage about grace illustrates, there is something that is graceful and grace-filled about Buechner's writing. As he draws us into his stories and helps us find something of ourselves in Theodore Nicolet, in Antonio Parr, in Leo Bebb, in Lucille, yes, and maybe even in John Turtle, the Joking Cousin, and Irma Reinwasser, I have the feeling that God's grace is slipping in around the edges and sometimes right down the middle.

LISTEN TO OUR LIVES, FOR ALL MOMENTS ARE KEY MOMENTS

That passage from *Now and Then* keeps recurring to me as crucial for Buechner. It is his way of prodding us toward the possibility of more abundant life. "Listen to your life," he says insistently and in many forms. "All moments are key moments" (*NT*, 92).

I don't take this in a terribly heavy sense of meaning that we must make life-and-death decisions every minute. At one point, to underscore the light, fantastic seriousness of life, he reminds us:

> We cannot live our lives constantly looking back, listening back, lest we be turned to pillars of longing and regret, but to live without listening at all is to live deaf to the fullness of the music. Somtimes we avoid listening for fear of what we may hear, sometimes for fear that we may hear nothing at all but the empty rattle of our own feet on the pavement.(*SJ*, 77–78)

Instead of heaviness or avoidance or fear, listening seems a way of lifting each moment up toward the sun, because we know it has the potential for meaning within it. Hidden within it are clues to what is really going on in our lives, treasure maps for discovering the meaning concealed in the strands of experience, magic spectacles for seeing something new about oneself and the world. Each moment is an opportunity to find and be found by God.

Brownie avoids listening by shoving his life under his rear end and sitting on it. Charlie Blaine sleeps in order not to be disturbed by any meaning that may intrude into his world. When Antonio takes Chris and Tony for a last visit to their mother, who is dying of cancer, she gives the younger boy a last word of advice. Antonio is telling us about it:

After she had kissed them goodbye and we were about to leave, Tony gave an enormous yawn, stretching one fat arm up into the air and knuckling his eyes with the other, and it seemed to rub her the wrong way because she sounded quite angry when she spoke to him and in some ways more like herself than I'd heard her for a long time. "Now you stay awake, Tony," she said. "You just keep your eyes open and stay *awake*."

There was a lot of life in her voice, a lot of Wop, and I can hear her saying it still. *Stay awake,* she told him as we left, and part of what she had in the back of her mind, I suppose, was poor Charlie with his naps and his kapok pillows sleeping his life away. *Stay awake* were the last words she spoke to my younger nephew and namesake, and looking back on it, not just the words but the fire inside them, what I think she meant was stay alive. "You just stay alive" was what she told that fat little boy with his zipper half unzipped, or there would be Hell to pay. And then we were gone. (*LC* in *BB*, 88–89)

Listening to our lives is no more or less than staying awake to what is going on around us. It means paying attention to the ordinary and maybe being ready to notice the extraordinary within what happens. For Buechner, that kind of listening and staying awake is what it means to stay alive.

LIFE EXPERIENCE PROVIDES METAPHORS TO REVITALIZE ART AND THEOLOGY

Buechner believes that both fiction and theology are, at the heart of both of them, autobiographical *and* metaphorical. To the extent that this insight is accurate, it offers a clue for imbuing both art and theology with new life. Only as each emerges from the experiences of our lives, takes images from human perception and deals with the enigmas and mysteries of human living, and has the purpose of helping us find meaning in the flow of events can either art or theology have that embeddedness in reality that is essential to their power.

And also, there is a continuing newness about experience. As artistic work and religious expression draw their metaphors from the concreteness of living, they are continuously renewed and have fresh and contemporary meanings about them. Such faith and art, therefore, remain capable of evoking interest, allegiance, and commitment in each emerging present because hidden within their innovative metaphors is the delicious bite of an ironic metaphysics.

Buechner is constantly providing illustrations of the potency of metaphors drawn from experience. It is the reason he is a breath of fresh air, opening long-closed windows, and therefore important for the Christian community today. He writes, for example, combining the old and the new:

> Faith is "the assurance of things hoped for, the conviction of things not seen," says the Epistle to the Hebrews (11:1). Faith is laughter at the promise of a child called laughter.
>
> If someone had come up to Jesus when he was on the cross and asked him if it hurt, he might have answered, like the man in the old joke, "Only when I laugh." But he wouldn't have been joking. Faith dies, as it lives, laughing. (*WT, 25*)

The other side of the matter is equally important for Buechner. The vitality of art and theology are necessary for human living. We need the images of art and the depth of theology to help us find our way in the maze of things that happen to us. Amazing maze and amazing grace! Stories drawn from experience that disclose some order present in the tangle of events can illumine our own lives and suggest some meaning, some plot, in the confusing things happening to us. Art and theology when they emerge from experience have the possibility of becoming chart and compass for those lost on watery wastelands of time.

Through the grace of one person's faith expressed in artful metaphors, the way appears and the lost become found.

GOD'S GRACE IS INCARNATE IN BOTH THE PROFOUND AND THE PROFANE

Throughout his writing Buechner challenges us to look again at all our attempts to distinguish sectors of life where God is present from those where God is assumed not to appear or at least seems absent. God is creator of all and is with us in all, even the most unlikely and despised places.

"The news of the Gospel is that extraordinary things happen," Buechner keeps saying to us in *Telling the Truth*. "Henry Ward Beecher cheats on his wife, his God, himself, but manages to keep on bringing the Gospel to life for people anyway, maybe even for himself" (*TT*, 7). And that seems to be the way God runs this world's railroad. Leo Bebb may or may not be all charlatan by intention but, by some twist of grace and irony, is a whole lot saint by the life he brings to people. Godric may have the more realistic view of himself and his unsaintly, checkered career, but he cannot shake off the impact of sainthood that somehow emanates from his life and that the pious Reginald is determined to chronicle no matter what unpious truths Godric tells him of the past or present. Like Leo Bebb, Godric is both fraud and minister of God. Sinner and saint are so inextricably compounded as to be inseparable, like wheat and chaff are until the winnowing. If my own experience and perception provide reliable clues, all that has the smell of truth about it.

I am, it seems, always in the midst of an ambivalence about my own life and experiences, knowing a little deliverance now and then, feeling a great deal of dereliction that seems to pervade all, and ever having a continual sense of delay. Like Godric, I suppose I tend to begin with delay, which gives rise to dereliction, and out of which comes yearning for deliverance. Why do some find deliverance and liberation along the way of life while others do not? Why do some people believe and others don't— or can't—or won't? We know no better answer than grace. And there may be no better answer. Indeed, perhaps there could be no better answer.

> By grace we are on that way. By grace there comes unbidden moments when we feel in our bones what it is like to be on that way. Our clay feet drag us to the bedroom of the garrulous old woman, to the alcoholic who for the tenth time has phoned to threaten suicide just as we are sitting down to supper. . . . We don't want to go. We go in fear of the terrible needs of the ones we go to. We go in fear of our own emptiness. . . . But we go because it is where his way leads us; and again and again we are blessed by our going in ways we can never anticipate. (*RCR*, 144–5)

THE GREAT LAUGHTER AFFIRMS/SUSTAINS LIFE THROUGH AND BEYOND SUFFERING AND TRAGEDY

"The worst returns to laughter," says a character in *Love Feast*, quoting *King Lear*. The worst thing is not the last thing—perhaps because there is yet laughter.

Buechner quotes again from Lear in *Telling the Truth*. It is a passage that comes after all the tragedy, misunderstanding, and waste have taken their toll on the bereft monarch: "Come, let's away to prison; / We two alone . . . / so that we'll live, / And pray, and sing, and tell old tales, and laugh" (*TT*, 72).

Central for Buechner's coming to self-awareness as a Christian was the notion that Jesus is crowned king among confession, and tears, and great laughter. He brings this experience to all his writing. Confession emerges in the actions of the characters in his novels, in the self-revelation of the autobiographical work, and in what we are called to in his sermons. But the lump in the throat that evokes the image of confession is also on the threshold of tears. As in a Chaplin movie, the tears are likely to be interrupted by laughter and the laughter stifled by renewed tears. In Buechner's art the three go together. But especially the laughter envelops the confession and tears so as to affirm and sustain life through and beyond all the suffering and tragedy that befall us.

Christopher Fry writes:

> There is an angle of experience where dark is distilled into light: either here or hereafter, in or out of tune: where our tragic fate finds itself with perfect pitch, and goes straight to the key which creation was composed in. And comedy serves and reaches out to this experience. It says, in effect, that, groaning as we may be, we move in the figure of a dance, and so moving, we trace the outline of the mystery.[29]

Buechner has this same sense of the inseparability and interpenetration of the tragic and the comic, not only in our experience, but also in the way we reach toward, and, in part, get some sense of, the meaning of the mystery that surrounds us no less through laughter than through suffering. The combination and the mutual illumination that takes places are the core of his art no less than his theology.

In *The Final Beast*, and with Nicolet, Buechner provides probably his most sensitive treatment of the comic that flits around the edges of the tragic and somehow winds up being a vehicle through which we are enabled to live through and maybe overcome tragedy. In the Bebb series the great laughter is at its most raucous and most healing point. And in *Telling the Truth*, he comes closest to letting us in on what he means.

Their shoulders shake. Their faces go red. Their china teeth slip a notch. She will be ninety-one on her next birthday, and the angel says she will celebrate it in the maternity ward. Sarah stuffs her apron in her mouth. Abraham gasps for air.

Then the question: Where does their laughter come from? It comes from as deep a place as tears come from, and in a way it comes from the same place. As much as tears do, it comes out of the darkness of the world where God is of all missing persons the most missed, except that it comes not as an ally of darkness but as its adversary, not as a symptom of darkness but as its antidote. The laughter of Abraham and Sarah at the angel's extraordinary announcement does not eliminate the darkness, because through the long, childless years of the past, darkness has already taken its toll, and in the long years that lie ahead there will be darkness for them still as, for instance, when Abraham is asked to take the child of the promise and offer him to God as a burnt offering. They both still have to face the darkness both of death and of life in a world where God is seen at best only from afar, through a glass darkly; but with their laughter something new breaks into their darkness, something so unexpected and preposterous and glad that they can only laugh at it in astonishment. (*TT*, 55–56)

So it is with all our living. The tragic will surely be there. But so also will be the laughter, with the magic of healing power that can sustain us in our suffering and give us a glimpse of what God has in store for us when we come to know that life itself is grace.

CONCLUSION

"All's Lost. All's Found. Farewell."

The last dying thought of the sinner/saint Godric focuses on the words "All's lost. All's found. Farewell" (*G*, 171). They provide for me the best context for concluding this account of my experience of Buechner. Perhaps they also suggest the most appropriate summary of Buechner's work. There is in these words much of Buechner's sense of the inclusiveness of grace and forgiveness. As we have seen, Buechner is indeed the novelist/theologian both of the lost and of the found, and he bids us to fare well on the journeys, the sacred journeys, that are our own lives.

But it is not enough to speak only of my journey or yours as though it were travel on a road that was safe and smooth, without hills or valleys or pain or peril. To be true to Buechner, we must understand the tension that is always and at every point a part of the journey. And then too, at the heart of this journey that is sacred, there is the mystery that both enshrouds and somehow illumines the way along which our travels take us.

ON THE ROAD

"In the middle of the journey of my life" Dante begins his *Divine Comedy*. So are we all in such a place. We are always in the midst of our living, somewhere on the way that is the journey of our life. "We're traveling on a road we've never seen before," says a song we sing sometimes in worship. The young people like it because they are just coming to full awareness of the uncertainties and the loneliness of the way. The older folks like the song because they find themselves looking toward the end of one life's journey and embarking on another that is really unknown. All those who are middle-aged have a different perspective and may be uninterested in the song or slightly impatient with it. They have known that the road has problems. They are not yet preoccupied with its ending, and they may be more concerned with getting on with the traveling than contemplating the meaning of the trip.

Buechner, with artistic vision and deftness, appeals to all three groups. He provides vivid images of the journey for those who are just discovering it for themselves. With stories that mirror the struggles of those caught in the middle and wondering whether anyone knows their pain, Buechner gently prods the middle-aged to become sensitive to their own pain and that of their companions along the way. And he affirms the memories and dreams of the old as they move toward the resolution of tension and approach the mystery that has surrounded them all along.

Buechner told his audience at Union Theological Seminary in Virginia

> If I were braver than I am, I would sing you a song. . . . But let me at least say you a song. It is from *The Lord of the Rings,* and Bilbo Baggins sings it. It goes like this.

> > The road goes ever on and on
> > Down from the door where it began.
> > Now far ahead the road has gone,
> > And I must follow if I can,
> > Pursuing it with weary feet,
> > Until it joins some larger way,
> > Where many paths and errands meet.
> > And whither then?
> > I cannot say.[30]

"'I am the way,' Jesus said. I am the road. And in some foolish fashion, we are all on the road that is his, that is he, or such at least is our hope and our prayer" (*RCR*, 143–4).

We're on the road, trying to get home. But, with Tip in *The Entrance to Porlock,* we ask, Where is home? Is it the place from which we started and to which we shall return, only to know the place for the first time? Or is it some unknown destination toward which we stumble through doubt and confusion? Or, perhaps, is the home we seek to be found in the journey itself? To the extent that Buechner is correct that the home we seek is to be found in Jesus as the way, then home is, in part, where we have come from and think we have lost; in part, also, home is the destination toward which we move even while thinking we are lost; and, in part, home is the pilgrimage itself in the midst of which we may lose ourselves and yet be wholly, holily found.

THE TENSION

"'The road goes ever on and on,' the song says, 'down from the door where it began,' and for each of us there was a different door, and we all have different tales to tell of where and when and how our journeys began," Buechner reminds us, and continues:

> Perhaps there was no single moment but rather a series of moments that together started us off. For me, there was hearing a drunken blasphemy in a bar. There was a dream where I found myself writing down a name which, though I couldn't remember it when I woke up, I knew was the true and secret name of everything that matters or could ever matter. As I lay on the grass one afternoon thinking that if ever I was going to know the truth in all its fullness, it was going to be then, there was a stirring in the air that made two apple branches strike against each other with a wooden clack, and I suspect that any more of the truth than that would have been the end of me instead of, as it turned out, part of the beginning." (*RCR*, 145–6)

To be in the middle of our lives most likely means not so much being aware of the journey as beginning, traveling, and ending as it means experiencing the potholes, obstacles, uncertainties, and too much ordinariness of the road.

We so desire to say it right, to do it right, to break through to the heart of reality. But who among us can? It is not so easy even to say it in a way that makes people experience our meaning, that moves them. Yet even doing that may only give the appearance of having a piece of reality in our grasp. It is so much harder to say it in a way that helps something happen within them that changes their world. "Come unto me." Can anybody except Jesus really say it right? Buechner knows that we must try with all our heart and mind and strength and artistic power. Yet the tension will remain between our actual efforts and what we hope for, between what we accomplish and what is needed. Still we try and hope and wait for the grace that makes our awkward attempts graceful, for the grace that makes the difference between the sense of lostness and the discovery that we have already been found.

H. Richard Niebuhr also uses the metaphor of a journey, a voyage on the ocean rather than travel by land. He reminds us that it is impossible to find final answers to the encompassing questions of history and human life. But there is a response we can make. He writes:

> Of course, every effort to answer these questions is relative to our own situation in this historical process of American faith and can claim for itself no more finality than can belong to that which is itself a part of the moving and shifting scene. Yet the sailor who seeks to find his bearings by consulting the charts his ancestors used when they set out on the voyage he is continuing, by noting all the corrections they have made upon them and by looking for the stars which gave them orientation may claim at least that he is trying to be true to the meaning of the voyage.[31]

All of us are wandering children of wanderers, as Buechner tells us in his storyteller's way. We yearn for freedom, for the feeling of being free—from oppression, from uncertainty and doubt, from sin and guilt, from the fear of death, and from death itself. In the midst of our yearning, we know that the exodus is happening. We have moments of discovering ourselves to be on the way of liberation, toward the land of promise. In those same moments of wild anticipation, we know that the wilderness is happening too. And we are lost in the midst of it, caught between hope for the promised liberation and fear that it has all been illusion. God brings each of us out of somewhere, toward a not-yet for which we wait. In the turmoil of our own wilderness, we may believe that the worst will not be the last thing, but there's plenty of trouble until the last arrives.

Each of us, could we find the voice, has strange and wondrous tales to tell. Within our experience we have been called to hear the voice of our own particular slavery, our own particular oppressions. The story we could tell also contains moments of liberation, steps on the way of exodus. And after each release there are new stretches of wilderness before us. Yet the deliverance is real too, and is ours.

We live in God's world of liberation, Buechner is saying. "For freedom, Christ has set us free" (Gal. 5:1). If we find ourselves enslaved, it is a bondage we ourselves have created. In our God-given freedom, it is often violence that we work. Our creativity bears the shape of the evil imaginations of the human heart. The lostness at times seems overwhelming. The demonic appears to permeate and threaten all our possibilities.

Does Jesus know me? See me? Am I really found or am I more alone on the road than even I know?

Why can't people love each other—as they are, for what they are?

Buechner explores these questions and, if he does not give us answers, at least helps us live into the questions. Because he is dealing with the great and ultimate enigmas of human living, some accuse Buechner of reducing people to stereotypes. That view is a misunderstanding of Buechner's characters. But it does represent, in distorted form, the important insight Buechner insistently suggests: perhaps all of us, in our different ways, are stereotypes looking for someone to set us free to authentic living. It is all too easy for us to let ourselves be pushed into the pigeonholes of our society and, shaped and confined by those confining spaces, to live out our lives without ever discovering the meaning of our journey. We may even cease to ask any of the big questions that nag at the heart of humanity. But we shall, through it all, not cease to complain about our fate as prisoners. If it is meaning we want, then Buechner may be able to help in liberating us from a stereotyped existence.

MYSTERY

"'And whither then?' Whither now? 'I cannot say,' the singer says, nor yet can I," writes Buechner. "But far ahead the road goes on anyway, and we must follow it if we can because it is our road, it is his road, it is the only road that matters when you come right down to it" (*RCR*, 149).

And then he tells a story:

I was sitting by the side of the road one day last fall. It was a dark time in my life. I was full of anxiety, full of fear and uncertainty. The world within seemed as shadowy as the world without. And then, as I sat there, I spotted a car coming down the road toward me with one of those license plates that you can get by paying a little extra with a word on it instead of just numbers and a letter or two. And of all the words the license plate might have had on it, the word it did have was the word T-R-U-S-T: TRUST. And as it came close enough for me to read, it became suddenly for me a word from on high, and I give it to you here as . . . a kind of present." (*RCR*, 149–50)

"Now we see in bits and pieces," might be the best English translation of Luther's German version of 1 Corinthians 13:12, "but then shall we see things in their wholeness." When is the *then* of that quotation? Shall we see the relation of things only in death? Will the wholeness disclose itself even then?

"What does it all mean?" we ask in puzzlement, often in despair, perhaps sometimes with a little hope. Surely this blooming, buzzing, wondrously enchanting world means something. How can all this struggle and turmoil and suffering and caring too much or too little not have some significance beyond being "a tale told by an idiot, full of sound and fury, signifying nothing"?

"No one *knows*," we must respond to these questions that well up out of our wayward longing. We are called to *trust*, not to *know*. And trusting is difficult for us. There are many lost people for Mr. Keen to trace, and much of the time I am one of them. But when someone affirms the possibility of God, of Jesus, it makes all the difference. Then I hear in the distance the thunder of the approach of the approach perhaps of horses and a cry, "Hi yo, Silver!" I'm not alone. I'm not crazy. And Buechner may just be right that the Christian story is too good not to be true.

This means that all our "knowing," if we know anything at all and if it can really be called knowing, is knowing by faith. In that way of knowing, which comes only through believing and trusting and hoping and loving, we can overcome the tension of the road and the uncertainty of the mystery.

Most of the time we escape only in part, from time to time, here and there, now and then. Suppose, though, that we could step into faith wholly, cast off from the anxiety of the tension, and dwell fully in the mystery. Suppose that we could learn really to *trust*. Is not this what the Gospel calls us to, and Buechner beckons us to perceive? Then we could cease living in Hell's suburbs, as we do so much of the time, and find a more fitting domicile for ourselves and our hopes.

And why not? I am here and might as well, through trust in God, make the most of it—being on my own particular journey, wrestling with and sometimes overcoming my own anxieties, in the midst of mystery. Perhaps I can even learn to say with Godric, "All's lost. All's found. Farewell."

After Nicolet's experience of "the approach of the approach perhaps of splendor" when he heard the clack-clack of the world's tongue as two apple branches "struck against each other with the limber clack of wood on wood," he attempts to explain it to the loyal but unimaginative Denbigh.

"I want you to listen to something. Just sit right where you are." Nicolet had risen to his feet and walked over to one of the trees as he spoke. "And listen."

Denbigh hooked his glasses back over his ears and craned around to see what Nicolet was doing. Nicolet took the ladder rung and gave one of the branches two sharp raps. . . .

"Could you dance to that?" he asked. . . . "If the life of faith was a dance, Denbigh, and this was the only music—all you could hear anyway—" with a few more double raps he began to suggest a kind of erratic rhythm "—do you think a man could dance it, Denbigh?"

"It sounds like calypso or something. I suppose you could dance to it," Denbigh said. "I'm not sure what you're talking about."

"I'm not sure what I'm talking about either." He tossed the rung toward the barn which it struck and fell. "But whatever this is we move through . . ." He raked his hand slowly back and forth through the air. "Reality . . . the air we breathe . . . this emptiness . . . If you could get hold of it by the corner somewhere, just slip your fingernail underneath and peel it back enough to find what's there behind it, I think you'd be—". . . .

"I think the dance that must go on back there," Nicolet began, "way down deep at the heart of space, where being comes from . . . There's dancing there, Denbigh. My kids have dreamed it. Emptiness is dancing there. The angels are dancing. And their feet scatter new worlds like dust." (*FB*, 180–2)

Perhaps we can get within the reality of our living enough to join the dance and find our feet taking us through the end of life, through death itself, into the eternal presence of God.

"I see a star," says Godric at the age of one hundred and more. "Sometimes this star is still. Sometimes she dances. She is Mary's star. Within that little pool of Wear she winks at me. I wink at her. The secret that we share I cannot tell in full. But this much I will tell. What's lost is nothing to what's found, and all the death that ever was, set next to life, would scarcely fill a cup" (*G*, 96).

With Godric and Buechner I am discovering that, when all is lost, all will be found, because the end of all our journeys is in God, with the dancing of stars and angels down the steeps at the heart of the world.

SO SAVE A DANCE FOR ME!

Afterword

As she mentioned in the preface, Margie experienced some strange symptoms while she was engaged in writing this book. It turned out to be a brain tumor. An operation on her and the report from the laboratory disclosed that the tumor was malignant. Further, it was the most aggressive kind, *glioblastoma multiforme*. That is the same form of cancer that John Gunther's son had back in the 1940s and that the elder Gunther wrote about so movingly in *Death, Be Not Proud*. We discovered that virtually no progress in finding an effective treatment had been made in almost forty years.

After the brain surgery, Margie had radiation therapy and, later, chemotherapy. None of these did more than delay the inevitable. With the help of one of the hospices that she had helped start, we found the support and the strength that enabled her to remain at home most of the time, in her own bedroom, surrounded by family, friends, and her beloved kitties. The tumor gradually expanded, reducing her ability to move, write, and speak, but never defeating her indomitable will and loving spirit. On Saturday, February 16, 1985, at 5:15 in the afternoon, Margie died.

In the early stages of her illness several people asked Margie, "Don't you ask 'Why me?'" She replied, with the same incredible trust and love that characterized all her life, "Why *not* me?" She had written a book in the early 1970s entitled *To Die With Style!* Through the process of writing it, she became prepared (we became prepared) for what we did not know then was to come. She had learned how to live toward her dying with consummate verve and style.

As long as she could write, she worked on this manuscript. After she could no longer make a pen do her bidding, we talked about particular parts that were not complete. And after she was no longer able to talk, I would discuss some points with her and she would respond with expressive facial movement or a squeeze of my hand.

With the encouragement of John Shopp, her editor at Harper & Row, and Fred Buechner, someone who became a dear friend to both of us, I have continued her work and completed the manuscript. It lacks the magic she would have given it with her wide-angle vision and dramatic style, but it carries out her carefully crafted intention and outline faithfully. Elizabeth Berryhill, who knew Margie's mind and spirit as well as anyone, Rosalie Moore, beloved friend and poet, and Dennis Roby, a former student of mine with keen literary and stylistic sensibility, helped with the tasks of looking up passages, following up Margie's notes and suggestions, and putting the finishing touches on a work that welled up from Margie's love of Buechner's writing and that has been brought to completion out of our love for her.

After her death I discovered, written in her own hand, a passage about the dance at the heart of the universe with a last line that sent me into tears and laughter. I decided that she meant it to go at the end of the text. She loved to dance and, if there was dancing at the heart of reality, she wanted an invitation. At the end of what, I think, was the last passage she wrote in her own hand for the book were these words: "So save a dance for me!" And that is what I call to her now, at the close of our efforts together to finish this book: "The party's not complete unless we waltz together in eternity. So, Margie, Margie, save a dance for me!"

Charles S. McCoy

Notes

1. Amos Wilder, "Strategies of the Christian Artist," *Christianity and Crisis* 25:7 (May 3, 1965): 92–95.
2. *Ibid.*, 92.
3. See H. Richard Niebuhr, *The Meaning of Revelation* (New York: Collier Macmillan, 1960), esp. p. x and ch. II, "The Story of Our Life."
4. J. F. Baker, *Publishers Weekly* 221:32–34, February 12, 1982, and *NT,* 59.
5. Paul Tillich, *The Courage to Be* (New Haven: Yale University Press, 1952), 46.
6. Alfred North Whitehead, *Religion in the Making* (New York: Macmillan, 1957), 144.
7. Wilder, "Strategies of the Christian Artist," 93.
8. Parker Palmer, *The Promise of Paradox* (South Bend, Ind.: Ave Maria Press, 1980), 46–47.
9. Amos Wilder, *Theology and Modern Literature* (Cambridge: Harvard University Press, 1958), 3.
10. Michael Polanyi, *Personal Knowledge: Towards a Post Critical Philosophy* (Chicago: University of Chicago Press, 1958), 198–99, and elsewhere.
11. Susanne K. Langer, *Problems of Art* (New York: Scribner, 1977), 23.
12. Roger S. Jones, *Physics as Metaphor* (New York: Meridien, 1983), 4.
13. Polanyi, *Personal Knowledge,* 199.
14. Wilder, *Theology and Modern Literature,* 7.
15. James Woelfel, "Frederick Buechner: The Novelist as Theologian," *Theology Today* 40:3 (October 1983): 290.
16. Shirley and Rudy Nelson, "Buechner: Novelist to 'Cultured Despisers,'" *Christianity Today* 25:10 (May 29, 1981): 44.
17. Sharon Gallagher and Jack Buckley, "A Conscious Remembering: An Interview with Frederick Buechner," *Radix Magazine* 15:1 (July/August 1983): 8.
18. *Ibid.*, 9.
19. Kenneth L. Gibble, "Listening to My Life: An Interview with Frederick Buechner," *The Christian Century* (November 16, 1983): 1042.
20. Charles S. McCoy, *When Gods Change: Hope for Theology* (Nashville: Abingdon, 1980), 37.
21. Niebuhr, *The Meaning of Revelation,* 35.
22. Rudolph L. Nelson, "'The Doors of Perception': Mystical Experience in Buechner's Fiction," *Southwest Review* 68:3 (Summer 1983): 266.
23. *Ibid.*, 268.
24. *Ibid.*, 270.
25. *Ibid.*, 271.
26. *Ibid.*, 272.
27. Tillich, *The Courage to Be,* 170–71.

28. Langer, *Problems of Art*, 26.
29. Christopher Fry, *The Dark Is Light Enough: a Winter Comedy*. New York and London: Oxford University Press, 1954. Printed on inside front jacket.
30. J. R. R. Tolkien, *The Fellowship of the Ring* (New York: Houghton Mifflin Company, 1965), 44.
31. H. Richard Niebuhr, *The Kingdom of God in America* (New York: Harper & Brothers, 1937), 15.

Index